tellwell

Tellwell Talent
www.tellwell.ca

ISBN
978-1-77302-996-2 (Paperback)
978-1-77302-997-9 (eBook)

SUBTEXT

A Whimsical Look at Men (Women too) and Manners

By

Sukumar Nayar

By the same author

The Vivid Air
(A memoir)

Published by Createspace
(Available through Amazon)

This book is dedicated to

NALINI NAYAR

my wife

my counsellor

my friend

my Muse

and

the mother of my children
Nikku and Radha

Everything in nature is lyrical in its ideal essence,
tragic in its fate and comic in its existence.

George Santayana

Life is a comedy for those who think;
a tragedy for those who feel.

Horace Walpole

ABOUT THE AUTHOR

Professor Sukumar Nayar has been my friend and occasional colleague for over 45 years.

When talking of Sukumar, it is difficult to know where to begin to describe his many qualities, abilities and achievements. He is an elegant, soft-spoken, delicate, immensely articulate and wise man.

Born, raised and educated in India at the height of the British Raj, he managed to gain advantage of the best of the British educational system. He gained Science, English and Education degrees at the University of Travancore and trained to be a teacher.

At this point his sense of adventure took over and he emigrated to be a teacher in Her Majesty's Service in Uganda, Africa, where he would become the Senior Master and Head of the Department of English at a Higher Secondary school, comparable to a Junior College in Canada. Uganda became independent of its masters, and the egregious Idi Amin became a dictator, who booted out many of the Asian Ugandans.

On arrival in Canada, he first became a teacher and then a Principal at a school in rural Alberta, then a lecturer and Chairman of Fine Arts at Grande Prairie Regional College in Alberta. He retired from the post-secondary system as the Northern Regional Director of Fairview College, Alberta.

His contributions in Grande Prairie in theatre are the stuff of legend. He made theatre happen in Grande Prairie.

About 1991 he began his very widespread international career when the United Nations hired him as a consultant in English, administration and theatre. His first appointment was to Ulan Bator, Mongolia. I remember getting a postcard to tell me that the program director there had died suddenly and he, Sukumar, had to take over the whole enterprise, which was to move the country from a controlled economy to a free market economy. His next assignment was to Papua New Guinea (PNG) to design an English language curriculum for the Higher Secondary system, reflecting PNG culture and values. After that it seemed that Sukumar had settled down and he contented himself with being a School Board Trustee.

At the turn of the century, though, his wanderlust returned and the Canadian Executive Services Organization (CESO) and the United Nations Development Program sent him to the Philippines and various cities in Russia to provide teaching and administrative help, and to organize performing arts festivals.

During all this time, Sukumar directed and produced over 150 theatrical productions. Everywhere he went he became the 'go-to' theatrical guru. Over the years Sukumar has tirelessly upgraded his skills in teaching and theatre arts at Universities in London, The Royal Academy of Dramatic Art in London, University of Montana and New York University.

His abilities have not gone unnoticed. He got a Distinguished Services Medal from the Government of Uganda, on the occasion of the country's independence though it should be remembered that they booted him out anyway. The Province of Alberta awarded him a gold medal in the millennial year. That year he also got "Theatre 100"—an award that was given to 100 theatre practitioners who had made a significant contribution to the development of theatre in Alberta over the past one hundred years. The city of Grande Prairie has also honoured him and he is a Professor Emeritus at Grande Prairie Regional College, where there is a large scholarship established in his name.

He has travelled to forty-one countries; he speaks six languages.

I know that his greatest joy is his marriage to Nalini, his charming wife of forever, and his two children, both of whom live nearby in Toronto.

Jack Wynters,
February 2017

FOREWORD

Humour inspired by insight and wisdom is rare, and so is a book that peers unabashedly at human foibles and helps us see them for what they are: absurd, astonishing, dangerous, and everything in between.

In this collection of essays, Professor Sukumar Nayar channels elements of the style of well-known humorists, across six themed, profusely illustrated sections, to reflect on his own incisive and often very funny look at the world around him.

Herein awaits a pithy peek at life, multiple musings informed by the author's decades of directing plays, teaching, parenting, consulting, and living around the world amongst the flawed mortals that we are.

In **"The Lighter Side"** readers will laugh and cringe at the trauma of airport passengers, reflect on the truth behind the saying, *older and wiser,* and marvel at the absurdity of having to annually prove oneself to be alive in order to satisfy the ridiculous requirements of some outdated policy handbook.

In **"Numbers"** the author quixotically indulges in his long fascination with digits, uncovering rarely-considered and clandestine meanings—and even numerical romance— from diverse cultures. You will be taken on a flight of fancy into the world of numbers from zero to ten.

"**Art**" gambols through various art forms, explaining, for example, how dance is the pastime of the Gods, to abstract paintings and the value we place (or not) upon them.

In "**The English Language**" the author——a self-professed "verbivore,"—luxuriates in the novelty, profundity, and exquisiteness of words in his most beloved language.

The penultimate section, "**Men (Women Too) and Manners**", defines the whole volume with its unvarnished examination of the vagaries of the human condition. A mixture of whimsy and sober second looks, it pokes fun of the habit of giving unusual names to children, at garage sales and burnout. He interrogates the habit of everyday insults, and explores the penchant for tattoos and ripped jeans.

Finally, "**The Darker Side**" probes into mankind's ominous urges and actions and outlines the dangerous futility of the ways that humans find to justify them.

In today's technology dominated, constantly rushing world, we need a book like this that takes us by the hand—and occasionally the nose—and makes us laugh and cry at our unvarnished selves. Professor Nayar is the ideal guide. He is an extraordinary, twinkle-eyed observer, a steadfast friend, and a great humanist who eternally hopes for, and believes in, a kinder, gentler world. This book is keyhole glimpse into both the man and all that we ought to think about.

Professor Christina Grant
University of Alberta,
Edmonton, Alberta
June 20, 2017

PREFACE

In 1999, the editor of **The Daily Herald Tribune** in Grande Prairie, Alberta, asked me if I would review the local theatre productions. Grande Prairie has a lively and vibrant theatre scene, and various amateur groups mount an average of one play every month.

I am a dramaturge by training and over the decades I have had running arguments and debates with friends and colleagues about the need for a review of community amateur productions. Who is the review for? Who does it benefit? Is the public better able to decide whether a show is worthy of their time and money after reading the review? What are the ramifications of a negative review? Or should all reviews be 'good'? Is the art form better served by a 'good' review, when a show by all accounts fails to measure up to basic and acceptable standards? Are there qualified critics in small communities?

During my long career, I have been almost exclusively involved in community theatre. My various casts and crews usually had little or no formal training. They were teachers, doctors, lawyers, butchers, shop keepers, bank clerks, housewives and such. For many of them it was a sacrifice because they had little time to commit to rehearsals and performances. All the same they participated for the sheer fun of it. Any negative comment would have only discouraged them from further involvement. Most of the participants were my friends and I did not want to hurt anyone's feelings and so I refused to review the plays. However, I offered to write on the performing arts scene in the city in the form of a column in the Friday Arts and Entertainment supplement of the paper.

Thus **Subtext** was born. Pretty soon I realized that there were not too many interesting things in the Arts & Entertainment field in the city to write about every week and so I veered off to other events and activities in the city, province, country and overseas. I touched on anything I thought would be interesting to a wider readership. The articles were innocuous, a whimsical look at men (women too) and manners, about life around us.

In 2009 I moved to Toronto and since no newspaper was interested in my articles, I started 'Subtext' as a weekly blog. Barring hiatuses caused by my United Nations assignments, family holidays and hospitalizations, I have been posting the blog every week.

One day in October last year, after reading the most recent blog, my wife suggested that, perhaps, I should pick a few of the 'better' ones and publish it as a book. My daughter who was sitting close by also vociferously supported the idea. In a weak moment I agreed.

When I looked at the archives, I realized that I had written over 620 articles and picking 52 of them—one for each week of the year—proved to be an onerous task.

While trying to pick the desired 52, I decided to sort them out into categories. I chose six: **The Lighter Side, Numbers, Art, The English Language, Men (Women Too) and Manners**, and **The Darker Side**.

The material and inspiration for many of the articles were provided by news outlets in Canada and elsewhere. I have also borrowed content for some of the articles from many sources like Wikipedia, opinions expressed by renowned columnists in newspapers, magazine articles etc. Obviously, I did a lot of 'googling'. As I have mentioned, the tone and tenor of most of the articles are by and large capricious, a light-hearted romp as it were, though I have included a few serious themes in the last section. Except in a few cases, I have used the first person singular, mostly indulging in a kind of self-deprecating humor.

I believe that there is material for two or three more books, but I had to be choosy to stay within the limits set by the publisher in terms of the optimal size for a paperback.

I wish to acknowledge the encouragement provided by family and a few friends. I thank Professor Christina Grant for writing the **Foreword** and Dr Jack Wynters, professional actor and retired physician, for introducing me to the readers.

I owe a special debt of gratitude to **Avijit Sarkar** of Sydney, Australia. He was kind enough to provide many of the images in the book. He designed the cover as well. Avijit is an exceptional individual. He is a concert musician, composer, puppeteer, and cartoonist among other things. He is also the editor of the e-zine called **The Mind Creative.**

I also thank my children Nikku and Radha who assisted in helping me pick the better ones from the mammoth list and patiently proof read the manuscript. Radha also had the unenviable job of formatting the manuscript into a pdf file and putting all the images in a jpeg file.

Finally, I also have to admit that the effort of compiling the articles was more challenging and time consuming than I thought. Many of the articles that I chose had been written years ago with local references. They were meant for a limited readership. Hence I had to enlarge the scope of the contents with an eye to making it interesting and relevant to an international readership.

But I am glad I did it.

Sukumar Nayar,
Toronto, June 20, 2017

CONTENTS

THE LIGHTER SIDE 3

NUMBERS 41

CONTENTS

The Darker Side 229

The Lighter Side

THE LIGHTER SIDE

I wonder how many people remember exactly when they reacted to something humorous for the first time. How old were you when you laughed at a joke or a funny situation?

When I was growing up, there were only three people in the house—my parents and myself. My father went to work in the morning and my mother took care of the chores in the house. By noon she would have a bath and after lunch snooze for a while and spend most of the afternoon reading, knitting or crocheting. But reading was her passion. Occasionally, while reading she would burst into laughter, and this was curious behavior for my very young self. Sometimes when father returned from work, over a cup of tea, she would talk to him and my father would start laughing. Later I understood that she was narrating to him the humorous part of the book she had been reading.

I vividly recall the first time I noticed something funny, something comical. This was when I went to see a movie for the first time. I was probably six years old. The movie had a mythological theme and I was engrossed in it. At one point a couple appeared on the scene and the crowd roared with laughter. It was as though they were expecting these two to appear. Their dress, dialect and general demeanor were unusual (to my eyes) and did not align with the rather serious theme of the movie (today I realize that they were doing a kind of Laurel and Hardy routine.) At one point after a bitter argument, the wife started beating the husband with a dead fish. I thought it was funny; I also joined in the laughter.

During my adolescent days, I used to participate in stage productions and many of them had 'humorous' lines, and it was with little difficulty that I realized that life is not all grim and heavy, but has lighter moments which sometimes evoke laughter.

Later on, G. K. Chesterton, Oscar Wilde, Anatole France, Jerome K Jerome, Moliere, Mark Twain, O.Henry, Stephen Leacock and others provided material which made me chuckle. But humor *a la* P.G.Wodehouse and Neil Simon was a different kettle of fish as the vernacular goes.

As Malcolm Jones said, "If you have not read a Wodehouse novel before and someone told you that it is about poker faced butlers, dotty aunts, elderly earls, and silly twits engaged in fay dialogue and plots filled with mistaken identities and foolish wagers and all the other feckless activities of the English upper class, you may not be interested in reading it. But that, as anyone who has read a Wodehouse novel will tell you, is merely what it is about. It's like saying that Moby Dick is a fish story. Wodehouse himself described his plots as musical comedies without the music, which might sound pretty dreadful, except that no one reads Wodehouse for the plot. You read them for the language and humor, which is more or less the same thing in his case." Neil Simon, on the other hand wrote humor to be spoken. And heard. He is a master of one liners. While you usually chuckle at a Wodehouse humor, you roar in laughter at Simon's writing. Item. "If no one ever took risks, Michelangelo would have painted the Sistine floor." Or "He's too nervous to kill himself. He wears his seatbelt at a drive-in movie."

Comedy is as old as civilization. We tend to associate Greek theatre with tragedy, but we know of only three major writers of serious plays—Aeschylus, Sophocles and Euripides. The known writers of Greek comedy are Menander and Aristophanes, but there were more than 200 playwrights who wrote the Satyr plays and other comedic work. The Greeks enjoyed their comedy. In terms of ancient Roman times, we have Plautus. Through the Middle Ages, the restoration period and into modern times, comedy has kept its legitimate place in literature and history. In addition to writing comedies, Shakespeare injected hilarity by introducing comedic characters or scenes to release the tension created by tragic episodes. The modern era saw Oscar Wilde, Bernard Shaw, James Thurber, Stephen Leacock and their contemporaries providing material guaranteed to tickle the funny bone.

We need comedy as a release valve because life around us has increasingly been taking on a sombre, indeed, depressing tone. **Punch, Shankar's Weekly** etc. were, during their time, eagerly sought out by readers. In many magazines jokes have become an integral part of the total package. When I get my copy of **Reader's Digest,** I first go to the jokes section. With **The New Yorker,** I first search for the cartoons. Thank God they exist.

SINE NOBILITATE

A very good friend of mine, a retired senior civil servant in India, appears to be vexed with an unusual problem. Recently he has started believing that he is a snob. He wanted to know if I agree with this characterization or not. I know why he asked me. He knows that I have been in the company of many snobs over the decades, in many countries and, as such, he thought that I would be able to recognize comparable traits in him. However, I could not do any long distance diagnosis and so I thought I would define a snob and describe snobbish behavior, a kind of checklist as it were, which he can use for self-diagnosis.

First of all, the origin of the word snob. It is derived from the habit, many years ago, of Oxford and Cambridge colleges writing *sine nobilitate* (without nobility) or s.n.o.b, next to the names of non-pedigreed students on exam lists and other documents. This was to distinguish them from their stuffy, aristocratic peers. Over time, popular culture has somehow reversed things, and now a snob is defined as "a person who strives to associate with those of higher social status and who behaves condescendingly to others."

At this point, I want to draw a distinction between 'posh' and 'snobbish'. Posh refers to a person of high class. Actually it is an acronym for 'Port Out, Starboard Home'. During the Raj, the Brits travelled to India by boat and the portside (the left side) was cooler than the starboard side. So the rich and the aristocrats had staterooms on the portside. Those rooms cost more too. But when the Brits returned, they chose cabins on the starboard side for the same reason.

A snob is not necessarily an aristocrat. Rather he is an ordinary Joe. He usually excels at name dropping. He would have met, personally known, or listened to celebrities. The intellectual snob is the person who quotes authors, especially classical writers, and says, "Plato said, did he not, that…" Note especially the rhetorical question, "Did he not?" inserted into the statement. He would have memorized lines from exotic poets like Gibran, Tagore or Omar Khayyam. He also knows everything about everything or at least has a strong view on everything.

The theatre snob would have seen the show you are talking about on Broadway or at the West End. At the very least, he would be able to quote from the reviews of the plays by reputable critics of the time. He also would have met or listened to celebrity actors, and more than likely would have a friend in the Royal Academy of Dramatic Art—RADA for short. In extreme cases he might even say that he had attended RADA as a student.

The art snob can be recognized by the quick look he gives to the pictures on your walls. His body language would suggest that you have poor taste in paintings. He might even be tempted to say something uncomplimentary like, "I hope you didn't pay an arm and a leg for *this*." It would pain him to say 'painting'.

In conversation, the snob often interjects with, "Speaking of…". You might be talking about the difficulty of getting a plumber or getting someone to landscape your yard or whatever. He would jump in saying, "Speaking of maintenance issues, I found it extremely difficult to get someone to renovate the kitchen in our condo in Hawaii." If you counter it with, "Jack, I did not know you *had* a condo in Hawaii!" he would give a sad look as if to say, "It is not easy being rich".

The snob is usually late in coming to meetings and parties. This is called 'being fashionably late'. He would breeze in, and interrupt the proceedings saying something like, "Sorry for being late. The wretched car would not start. And I paid $86,000 for it, believe it or not." (We believe you, pal, we do.) In a group, if a person uses the word 'astonishing' instead of 'unbelievable' or 'surprising' you have a snob in your midst. He would prefer to use 'although' instead of the mundane 'though'.

You have to be very careful inviting a snob to a party in your house. For one thing, as I have already mentioned, he would come late and will have a very credible excuse. You would probably ask whether you could get him something to drink. He would say, "Give me some Balvenie 25 ($410), *if you have*." You see, he knows that you don't stock expensive single malt whisky. So you would probably say that you have

Johnny Walker Blue ($182). He would dismiss it and say, "Give me some ginger-ale then." The subtext is clear!

I just decided to look back at what I have written so far and I realize with a shock that I am actually *describing myself*—my own linguistic and behavioral habits! Hmmm. Well, I'll let my friend figure that out for himself.

BLAME IT ON MY PHIZZOG

In the story **My Financial Career**, Canadian humorist Stephen Leacock talks about a man who got rattled whenever he went to the bank. Clerks at the wickets frightened him.

I have a similar problem whenever I enter the immigration hall in an international airport. And I have been through quite a few!

To explain. The moment I cross the red line and present my passport, declaration forms and such, the expression on the faces of the officer changes. I am subjected to more than the usual barrage of questions.

Of course, I blame it on my face or as Carl Sandberg called it, 'my phizzog'.

To avoid unpleasantness, I have spent a lot of time thinking about how to reduce the trauma. To that effect, many years ago, I made a practice of staying back before rushing to join the line. Then I would survey the faces of the uniformed public servants (servants? Bah!!) and pick one who has not forgotten to smile. You know, a person who does not appear to suffer from bouts of dyspepsia. Then taking comfort in the fact that I have picked a friendly keeper of the gate, I would flash a big smile (easy with my big mouth) and greet this individual. But the moment we make eye contact, the hitherto smiling face would get sullied by dark clouds and the questions follow. They always find something wrong.

Those who have read my memoir (**The Vivid Air**, available from Amazon) would recall how I nearly got incarcerated in Athens because the authorities thought that I looked like a Turkish Cypriot terrorist! I don't always elicit (or is it provoke?) such strong responses. But detailed (and, in my opinion, totally unnecessary) inquisition? Yes.

A few years ago, I was on my way home from a United Nations assignment in the Philippines and I landed in Vancouver. I had approximately twenty five dollars' worth of stuff to declare. One of them happened to be a handbag made of straw. As usual, I made my nervous trek to the red line, and as soon as I crossed it, I noticed that the officer who had hitherto been smiling put on a grave appearance.

He scanned the declaration form with a frown on his face and noticed that I had declared the bag. He was very curious about the bag. "What kind of straw?" I said, "Straw is straw. It is a plant product. Dried leaf, in fact."

This was meant to be humorous, but he was not amused!

"You are sure you have only 25 dollars' worth of stuff to declare?" I said, "Yes." "Well, you better report to the

agriculture department; they might have to quarantine….."
The last word or phrase was inaudible.

So I collected my bags and walked around looking for the agriculture person. Finally I spotted the bench. A thirty something youngster was flirting with one of his colleagues. They were obviously not busy. Who is going to smuggle plant products without authorization?! Anyway, starved for excitement, he was licking his lips in anticipation when he saw me trotting up to the bench. Of course, the pleasant expression vanished in a flash. Stanislavsky would have been proud.

I explained the situation but had to open my suitcase to show the wretched bag! When he saw what I had, his expression changed to incredulity and, perhaps, disappointment in not being able to nail a potential smuggler of taro root or the foul smelling durian! After a moment of hesitation, the fellow proclaimed, "I don't know why they sent you here!"

"It's my face," I replied.

One has to wonder about these people, though. In 1982, John Zaritsky, a Canadian, won an Oscar for the best documentary film, **Just Another Missing Kid**. To the question millions of passengers have heard from thousands of customs officials, he said, "Only an Oscar!" I believe he was trying to be funny. He probably was trying to imitate Oscar Wilde. When he arrived in the United States, to the question if he had anything to declare, Wilde said, "Only my genius!"

Getting back to Zaritksy, the officer wanted to know what the Oscar actually was and how much it was worth! Zaritsky was clearly baffled. He said that he had no idea. "It is just a statuette, gold—" He had no time to say 'golden'. The officer roared, "How much gold? What did you pay for it?"

How much **is** an Oscar statuette worth?! Then he remembered that he had signed a document which committed him never to sell his award for more than 10 dollars.

"Er, the monetary value is 10 dollars," he said. "American or Canadian?" asked the officer. He also wanted to know where he purchased it and whether he had a receipt to prove its value. I believe the officer settled for a $12 value and Zaritsky paid duty on that!

Image Credit: Newsday

SAY WHAT?

My wife and daughter are vegetarians. My daughter, who has taken domicile in our apartment ever since I returned from my incarceration in the body shop (a.k.a Mount Sinai Hospital) recently, announced the other day that supper that night would be spaghetti and meat sauce. I raised my eyebrows a bit like Jeeves used to when he heard goofy statements from his employer Bertie Wooster. But Jeeves's eyebrows rose only a mere half an inch. Wodehouse was very clear on that. Mine, on the other hand, went up a clear inch. Obviously. It appears my daughter read my confusion and clarified the matter. She was going to use 'vegetarian beef'.

Say what?!

To put my mind at rest she produced a packet which looked like ground beef, and I admit the final product did taste like beef. Gourmands know that I am talking about soy products. But it is almost as though soy is masquerading as beef! One is reminded of animals using camouflage for protection.

Using an oxymoron is nothing new. Shakespeare used them many times. In one of his sonnets he talks about

lascivious grace. 'Lascivious' is synonymous with prurient, smutty and ribald. Relating this with 'grace' is the ultimate contradiction. But the Bard used words with impunity. If he could not think of a word, he invented one. Scholars believe that there are close to 1700 words in currency now, attributable to the Bard's inventive genius. 'Bloody', 'misplaced', 'ribald', and 'sanctimonious' were never part of the vocabulary of Elizabethans until Shakespeare invented them. Imagine, someone actually creating a word like 'sanctimonious'!!

Of course, Shakespeare is not the only verbivore (logophile if you prefer) that had used oxymorons. Oscar Wilde famously said, "I can believe in anything, provided it is quite incredible." Mark Twain could "resist everything but temptation." Andy Warhol in his own words was a "deeply superficial person."

The fact is that every day we use many expressions that could be easily be classified as a contradiction in terms.

We associate burn with fire and freezing with excessive cooling. But we also talk about **freezer burn. Thunderous silence** is a blatant insult of Zeus. Perhaps this expression inspired Simon of the Simon & Garfunkel duo to compose the song **Sounds of Silence.** During the many seminars that I have attended, the speaker used to say, "**Now, then.**" Beats me! I have heard people say that something is **pretty ugly.**

I was a motorcycle aficionado and at one time I had toyed with the idea of joining that admirable organization called **Hells Angels.** But I did not have the brawn on my frame to qualify. Also I am averse to tattoos disfiguring my body.

I have heard many people refer to **open secrets**. Anthony Haden Guest, the British-American writer, reporter, art critic and socialite admitted that, "He could certainly keep secrets but it was the people he tells them to, that can't keep them." The other day one of my friends was trying to clarify the use of a certain software for my computer. After many frustrated efforts he declared that I was **clearly confused.** Charlie Brown gave the expression **good grief** a new dimension. And someone, please explain to me what **same difference** means.

There are certain things I simply cannot do. When I was a student at the Royal Academy of Dramatic Arts in London, I was asked to demonstrate a **sad smile**. I couldn't, which, perhaps, explains why I flunked the Acting course. The **only choice** left was to withdraw from the theatre program. But I do have many **bittersweet** memories of my brief stint at that venerable institution.

To save laundry bills we routinely use **paper table cloths** on our dining table. And after supper, washing up is my portfolio and for greasy pots I always use **steel wool.**

Say what?

MIND OVER MATTER

People who know me also know that I have a dour disposition. I am—and have been—cantankerous by nature. I have a short fuse, and a caustic sense of humor. All qualities totally unsuitable for someone who wanted to pursue a career as a social worker.

In a word, utterly disagreeable. Well, two words.

When I moved to Canada from Uganda, a friendly shrink strongly suggested that what I needed (desperately, he said, for added emphasis) was to clean up my mind. Give it a thorough scrub, as it were. He recommended Transcendental Meditation. TM for short.

This was in the late seventies, and TM was just making its presence known on the continent. There were many centres operated by people who claimed to have been inducted by the great one—Maharishi Mahesh Yogi. But I wanted the real stuff and so trekked to San Francisco when I heard that His Holiness would be there for a few months. Nothing like going right to the fount! When I got there, I was told that it was not possible to see the head poohbah, but one of his disciples would be happy to oblige for a mere $1,000 dollars.

In those days it was a steep price to pay for laundering your mind. I had an old aunt, who had a sure-fire cure for almost any erratic behavior. For instance, when I was a small boy, I had the habit of sleep walking. She recommended to my worried mother that what she needed to do was to make me sleep under the cot. My mother took her advice. It took only two nights and an equal number of nasty bumps on the head to cure me!! But, alas, the aunt is no longer with us, and I had no recourse but to depend on the yogis for help.

First I had to register before a minor yogi—possibly an intern—and after a while I was escorted to a room, which had mood lighting. There was the smell of incense and a yogi was sitting in the centre. He was a big fellow with a forbidding mien. Looked like an overweight Basil Rathbone with long hair and beard. He had an aquiline nose and a pair of enormous eyes.

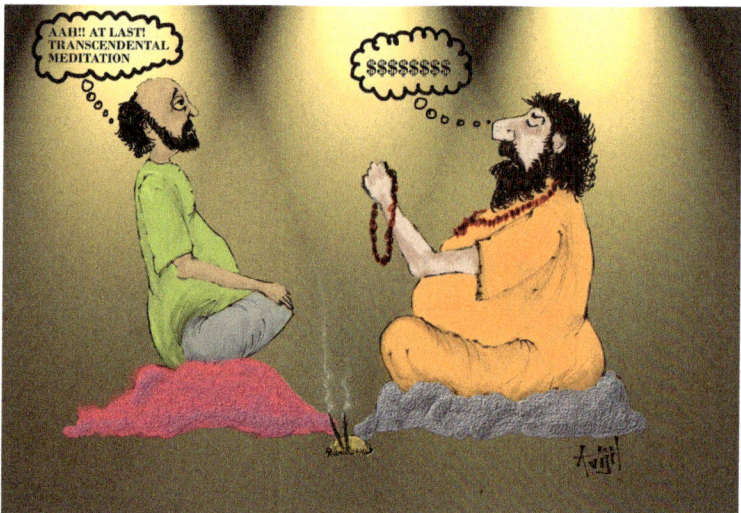

His name was Mrishtanna Bhojanaananda Swami. In Sanskrit it means a swami who likes a hearty meal, with a variety of dessert dishes thrown in.

He listened to me patiently and said that he would give me a personal 'mantra'. "Nobody in the world knows this except the two of us." So it was unique. The word was **'chimp'**. I had to sit in a darkened room, assume the lotus position, light an incense stick, close my eyes and silently chant the word, with total concentration. "Think of nothing else, not even the monkey." (This last, he said, would improve my powers of concentration. Absolute control of the mind follows.) I was able to do that, I would be on the path to recovery. "How long would it take?" I asked. "Ah, my son", (He was much younger than me, by the way. But I chose to ignore the slight) **"that** depends on you. Come next year and talk to me."

Anyway what happened after my bout with TM is not of any consequence. Did I get a good cleansing? Hardly. Did I go back? No.

That was then. Now, in my old age, it seems that I am exhibiting the same traits that led to my downfall as a social worker. I am a grouchy old goat. At least, the family has been reminding me of this.

Naturally, I felt upset and concerned on hearing this feedback from the *familia*. I called my friend Dr. Titus Mathews in Calgary to get his professional advice. He suggested that what I needed to do was to practise yoga. And I was thrilled to learn that a yoga teacher came and held sessions every week in our apartment.

So I went to see her. She was quite enthusiastic. But I needed to get a yoga mat and Lulu Lemon yoga pants. You know, the basic equipment. She told me where to get them. $150, if you are curious.

Anyway, I went to the first session, all gung-ho! I went early and noticed that there were a few chairs against the wall. For spectators, I told myself. The members drifted in twos and threes. A few people came and sat on the chairs, I noticed. Going to yoga gives you a special aura as it were…walking around with the mat rolled up in your arm and wearing the costume. People look at you and whisper with reverence, saying "Don't look now. That short old man who clearly has arthritis in his legs goes to yoga classes." At the appointed hour the teacher walked in and I was introduced as the newest member.

I was asked to put the mat on the floor and squat. If possible, I was to assume the lotus position. Well, I have done a lot of stupid things in my life, but this, as the Bard said was *nonpareil.* I did as I was told and something cracked, (I later realized that they were my knees, both of them) and it appeared as though the noise reverberated in the room. I was wincing with pain.

Now there was a small problem of getting up because any activity on the mat was clearly out of the question. The word 'chimp' *flashed upon that inward eye.* The same flash that Wordsworth got when he was *in a vacant or pensive mood.* I got up and chose to spend the rest of the session sitting on a chair.

After the mandatory one and a half hours, during which I just went through the motions, I came home limping. The wife, who was immersed in reading the newspaper, asked me how the session went. I gave a brief description and declared my intention to discontinue.

"Well, take a cold shower when you get the urge to be miserable," she said sagely.

Some sage!

CURLING

As I have mentioned in the previous article, I am a sour puss and a grouch. I don't generally smile, but that is because I have bad teeth like Josephine Bonaparte or Mona Lisa. I know, I know, one does not have to bare the fangs when smiling. I also admit that my eyebrows are in a knitted state very often. It is this feature, I assume, that has generated the impression about me. It has nothing to do with my character or temperament. It is just that I am always confounded by many things that go on around me. Inexplicable things. And when I try to figure them out, I have this expression on my face.

Take the game of curling for instance. I consider myself a sports buff, but curling is a real head scratcher. How could anyone club it together with tennis, soccer and similar sports?

For the benefit of my readers in Mongolia, Abu Dhabi, Chad, etc., who may not know what the game is about, may I seek the indulgence of connoisseurs of the 'sport' and describe it?

The Canadian humorist Eric Nicol, I believe, defined it as a refrigerated form of lawn bowling. Canadians, especially in Prairie towns with names like Moose Jaw, Pain Court,

Eyebrow, Medicine Hat, or Bacon Ridge might believe that this is a Canadian game. They would be wrong. In fact it actually originated in Scotland—like golf.

According to legend a young highland bride was baking her first haggis for her husband. When she took it out of the oven it fell from her hands. Here history gets a bit confused. One version is that it actually fell on the leg of the husband, cutting it off at the ankle. The other version is that it went through the floor into the cellar below. Whatever the truth, the Scot, being of a frugal nature, stuck a handle on the haggis and took it out on the icy street and rolled it. And the game of curling was born.

But now the game is on a sheet of ice called the 'rink' measuring 19m x 5m. Not icy streets. The participants are perfectly normal looking people, four in each team. They stand at each end of the rink and proceed to *throw* a rock at one another. This rock weighs 44 pounds, and hence the danger of rupturing the internal organs.

The objective of the game is to *throw* the rock to the other end of the rink. Of course, you cannot actually *throw* the rock. It is hyperbole of the first order. Even Olympian shot putters are given a ball weighing only 16 pounds. You slide the rock down the rink. However, before you slide it, in order to gather momentum, you have to swing the arm (which is attached to the rock) as far back as possible. The duodenum snaps, and presto! You get a hernia!

After a rock is thrown, two members of the team follow it, bending down, cooing and encouraging it to accelerate.

In this effort they also use a broom (a brush these days) to sweep the area just in front of the rock to clear any debris that might have found its way on the rink. Then you might hear two furious guttural instructions from another member of the team. These noises sound like 'hayerrrddd' and 'woe, woe, woe'. The first sound is an instruction for the sweepers to sweep, you guessed it, hard. Faster. Responding to this order only aggravates the hernia. Obviously, the second is to slow down. One more important fact. When the rock is released, the curler gives a gentle twist of the handle before releasing it and so the rock 'curls' during its short journey to the other end.

All this hard work is to ensure that the rock is where it is supposed to be. The only problem is that the opposition will have their turn and knock it off. So it is conceivable that at the end of one session, there is no score at all. It is as silly as a five day cricket match, where 22 players, dressed in white, toil from 10 in the morning to 5 in the afternoon for five days, only for the umpire to declare a draw.

By the way, I am not convinced that sweeping is necessary at all. If the player is talented enough, he should be able to control the speed of throwing, so that the rock reaches exactly where it is supposed to reach.

I know aficionados of the game will call for my blood!

OLDER THE WISER? POPPYCOCK

Aesop, the Greek writer of fables, is said to be the first person to have bestowed on the owl the status of the wisest member of the animal kingdom. Later on A.A. Milne in **Winnie the Pooh** would confirm this. Human beings, alas, don't have a "go-to" symbol of sagacity. The closest we have is a conventional belief that as we get older we get wiser, meaning that if you are looking for wisdom, you should go to an old man.

I don't know who the idiot was that concocted this. The axiom means that we learn more as we grow older and are better able to understand the world around us than when we were, say, twenty. I have not reached Lincoln's 'four score and seven', though I am getting there slowly and unsteadily. But lately I am beginning to wonder if the

SUBTEXT

truism about old age and knowledge is valid at all. I have noticed that there are many things that I don't understand or know about, while others around me seem to.

For instance, I don't understand why we have to insert coins to extricate luggage carts at airports. It is very unfair of the authorities to expect a man from Burkina Faso to carry dollar coins before boarding the plane bound for Toronto. Or a man from Sydney, Australia, to have dollar bills in his wallet when travelling to Los Angeles. He probably would carry traveller's cheques with the idea of converting them into local currency once he gets to a currency exchange, but the exchange kiosks are outside the luggage carousal hall. Sometimes even when you put the coins in the slot, removing the cart becomes a tug of war because the cart you want is inextricably stuck with the one ahead of it! No, I don't understand this at all.

I don't understand why we park on the drive way and drive on the parkway. I asked a couple of wiser, not necessarily older, people (at least they appeared to be wise) for an explanation. They had no clue.

I don't understand why some of the business people say, "*Thank you, kindly.*" after a transaction. In 1965, when we emigrated from Africa, our first port of call in Canada was Vancouver. After checking into a hotel, I went out to buy a few things, and when I paid the shop keeper, he said, "Thank you, kindly." Not having been familiar with the expression, I must admit that I was confused a bit. On the way back to the hotel, being a linguist, I tried to analyze the statement. I did not know where the element of kindness figured in the transaction.

I gave him the money, he gave me the merchandise. I think he was the one who showed kindness. He could easily have refused to serve me for any number of reasons: my height or lack of it, my external appearance, or whatever. No, I don't understand the usage at all.

I don't understand how we **catch a cold** while we **have a fever** or **get a fever**. I have not heard anyone tell me, "I am sorry, I have caught a fever and so I cannot come to the rehearsal." You see, 'catch' implies motion. You can't catch, say, a stapler on the desk. You catch a ball coming at you or you catch a falling star. But you don't 'catch' a cold. You don't catch germs on the fly and stuff them in your nostrils. Do we catch arthritis?

And I certainly don't understand the use of the word **terrific**. I asked a friend what he thought of the play **Matilda**, which had successful runs all over the world. He said, "It is a terrific play; you must see it." I decided to go back to the root of the word and I discovered that it is derived from the French word '*terrere*' meaning to '*frighten*'. As far as I know, the play is about a seven year old girl, not even remotely terrifying. No, I don't understand this at all.

The monstrous amount of things that I don't know would require a book and not a mere essay. But I do feel constrained to make mention of one more item, a statement that is heard these days in my house pretty much on a regular basis. That is: "You look like you got out of the wrong side of the bed again." The subtext is that I am grouchy on certain days. Well, I can't help it. Some are born grouchy; some acquire grouchiness over the years. I am a born grouch. But even if I were not, there is no credible research to prove any correlation between grouchiness and the side of the bed you stumble out of in the morning.

The more I think and write, the more I am convinced that my ignorance is near abysmal. I would like to rectify this. Go to Google, you say? Well, with the limitations I have in understanding the intricacies of the computer, I would be better off staying ignorant.

Of course, I could get an owl as a pet. Maybe it could help me figure things out.

DEAD OR ALIVE? PROVE IT!

Before moving to Canada, I was employed by the British Government in Uganda and for my services the Crown gives me (still!) a monthly pension. However, every year I have to fill out a form and swear before a Commissioner of Oaths or a Lawyer, an affidavit that I am actually alive, and that I am, indeed, the same person who had left the Colonial Service in 1965.

Not an unreasonable demand, I must say. The Queen, already strapped for cash for sensible expenditures like fixing the leaky roof and broken plumbing in Buckingham Palace, does not want to give a pension to someone who has been buried (or cremated) years ago. Obviously.

But this cannot be said of the affairs in the 'land of the free and home of the brave'. The US government has a problem with dead people. For one thing, it pays them way too much money!

Or so says David Fahrenthold of **The Washington Post.** According to him, in the past few years, Social Security paid $133 million to beneficiaries who were deceased! The federal employee retirement system paid more than $400 million to retirees who had passed away! And an aid program spent $3.9 million in federal money to pay heating and air-conditioning bills for more than 11,000 people who were already dead.

These mistakes are due to screw-ups at the federal level. An outdated jury system meant to track deaths has trouble determining which Americans are deceased.

As a result there are two issues: the living dead and the dead living!

As Fahrenthold says, "The first group consists of people who have died but the records show that they are alive. Millions of dollars pile up in unwatched accounts. In one recent record breaking case, a son stole his dead father's federal benefits for 26 years. In 1995 the government sent a letter to a federal retiree named Silas McHenry Sr. It came back signed—by Silas McHenry Jr. The Junior McHenry assured the government that his father was alive but afflicted by Alzheimer's disease. The same thing happened in 1997. And in 2005. But in 2009 a fraud inspector called to make sure that the elder McHenry was still alive. He wasn't. By that time junior had stolen 26 years of his father's benefits, at least $1.1 million! When he was caught he pleaded guilty and was sentenced to 4 years in a federal prison.

The second group consists of living Americans—at least 750 new people every month—whom the system falsely lists as dead! This is really hilarious because once you are on the list, it is not easy to get off. Last summer in Utah a man went to the Social Security Office to prove that he was, indeed, very much alive."

I can imagine how the scene might have developed. He walks into the office and is greeted, not too warmly, by someone who is clearly suffering from peptic ulcer.

"Yeah, what can I do for you?"

"Apparently my federal records show that I am dead. I am here to prove that I am not and that I am very much alive."

"You will have to fill out a form, but before submitting it, you must undergo a medical examination by our resident doctor."

"So, what kind of examination is this?"

"I don't know. I am not a doctor."

"So, how do I get to see the doctor?"

"You have to make an appointment. He works only on Mondays, Wednesdays and Fridays."

"So, can I make an appointment now that I am here? When would he be available?"

"You will have to talk to his nurse about it. I cannot give appointments for the doctor. My job is to accept the applications and send them for processing. In any event he has gone home for the day."

"But it is only two o'clock."

"So I see. There is nothing I can do about that."

"May I ask you a silly question?"

"Go ahead. It is a free country."

"Surely you can see that I am not dead. I am a living, breathing human being like you. Why do you have to harass me like this?"

"Listen grandpa, I did not make the rules. Look, I had a very bad day. Please don't make it any worse. Why can't you guys stay dead and not bother us?"

The names of dead people are in the **Death Master File** kept in the offices of the Social Security Administration. Every day new reports are added, provided by relatives, funeral homes, and the state agencies that issue official death certificates. The list contains approximately 90 million reports. The problem is that not all of them are correct. And as I have mentioned, once your name gets on the file, it is extremely difficult to remove it.

The task of tracking deaths is onerous. Approximately 2.5 million Americans die every year, and the officials say that vast majority of cases are handled correctly. But not always. "In 2011 alone, the auditors found that Medicare paid $23 million for services *provided* to dead people. From 2009 to 2011, it spent $8.2 million on medical equipment *prescribed* by doctors to people who had been dead for at least a year," says Fahrenthold.

Numbers

NUMBERS

I shudder to think of where we would be if man had not invented the concept of numbers. Numerical notations existed long before the invention of script, and archaeologists suggest that at least 30,000 years ago man used notches as primitive, numerical representations for things.

We use numbers without thinking much about them. It is more or less a routine affair. Date of birth, the ten o'clock news, 2 per cent homogenized milk, the elevator button to take us to our apartment, the 3.12 train from Paddington (3.15 would have been more logical, but!), 911…

Sometimes numbers are used in a 'spiritual' context. 13, for instance, is unlucky in certain cultures. In China many numbers are considered auspicious. Number 8 for instance.

Do numbers have anything to do with language? Yes, they do. At least, according to German linguist Heike Wiese. In her most interesting book **Numbers, Language and the Human Mind**, Wiese demonstrates the relationship between numerical thinking and the human language faculty. Any discussion at any level on this is beyond the scope of this introduction. But there is no question how much numbers have influenced our daily use of English. I am going on a flight of fancy into the world of numbers zero to ten and I invite you to join me.

0

No matter what you call it: **goose egg, duck** (as in cricket), **love** (as in tennis) **Ciphra** (Latin), **Babu** (Hausa), **Nula**(Czech), **Sifr** (Pushto), **Meithen**(Greek), **Noll** (Swedish), **Shunya** (Sanskrit) or **Zero** , it means the same thing – nada, zilch, zip, naught. Nothing.

Most scholars agree that the number **Zero** and the circular symbol that represents it originated in India. It had its root in Vedic literature which is nearly 4000 years old. Between 1000 BCE and 1000 AD, various treatises on mathematics were authored by Indian mathematicians, in which were set forth, for the first time, the concept of zero. They called it 'shunya' meaning nothing, as mentioned above. **Shunyata** is a profound Buddhist concept. It means emptiness, the void, the essence of all things, the mother of all existence from which everything is born and into which everything must return.

The Arabs borrowed the idea and brought it to Baghdad, from where it went to Spain. Europeans changed the name to zero.

You put a cardinal number after it; zero spurns it with the hauteur of a dowager. But you put it behind and it is an entirely different matter. It gains importance and strength as though through some osmotic process. More zeros mean more power, which increases exponentially. A lowly number one with just five zeroes after it takes on a totally different character with the addition of one more shunya, babu, ciphra or whatever.

For some people adding another zero to their emoluments is not all that difficult. The top players of football, baseball, basketball and tennis for example. Or the top musicians. Or the top hedge fund managers. Or Leonardo DiCaprio, who is reportedly paid 77 followed by 6 zeros for every movie that he makes. You take one zero out, and he instantly becomes poorer. Take out five more and he becomes destitute. Such is the power of zero!

Computer programmers are virtually impotent without zero. Computers are full of zillions of numbers – lots and lots of ones and zeros. When you type the letter "A", the computer representation is 0100001. I don't understand this. I wonder how many zeros and ones are required to represent this paragraph!

Now guys who have scant respect for zero are astronomers. For them half a dozen zeros more or less make no difference. They deal with astronomical figures (the pun is not intended). For instance they claim that the Andromeda Galaxy is 21,759,680,086,935,840,000 km away. Give or take a couple of zeros! Since it is humanly impossible to deal with so many zeros in common parlance, the astrologers, to make our life easier, say that the same Galaxy is 2.1 million light years away. And a light year is the distance equivalent to the distance light travels in one year which is nearly 6 trillion miles. And light moves at a velocity of about 300,000 km each second.

I am sure you get the drift.

Of all the mathematical symbols, zero is the most elegant and sensual. The triangle has sharp points, and the square is, well, square. The zero represents the perfect circle. (I know, I know, people are known to make them oval shaped. Sacrilege, if you ask me.) It has a cosmic beauty. Consider the shape of a full moon or a setting sun. It is the epitome of perfection. Like eternity, it has no beginning, no end.

One would think that with all the glamor surrounding it, all people would like it. Not the cricketer. Nothing scares the batsman more than scoring zero and leaving the field in ignominy. In technical lingo it is called a 'duck'. Many batsmen who had scored a duck in both innings are known to have contemplated suicide. While on the theme of sports, in tennis the zero score is called 'love'. In other words at the beginning of the match, the umpire calls 'love all', a suggestion which is promptly dismissed, especially when players like Djokovic, Nadal and Raonic turn the tennis court into an arena reminiscent of the glory days of Caligula and his gladiators. They fight until 'death do us part'. 'Love' is soon forgotten. Going for the jugular becomes the call of the day.

It is irritating to see people use the term for less than noble purposes. For instance, I don't like the term **zero tolerance**. 'No tolerance' would have been sufficient. 'Absolutely no tolerance' has even more potency. It is hilarious that some sour grammarian, probably suffering from a migraine while trying to make sense out of English grammar coincd the term **zero article** to refer to the absence of a definite article (a, an, the) before a noun. What rubbish!

And the ultimate obscenity? **Zero balancing**! I could have accepted it, with reluctance, if it had anything to do with accounting. No. It is *'a manual therapy in which the practitioner applies finger pressure or traction to tense tissue to enable relaxation and reorganization'*. It has been described as *'a bodywork modality that claims to balance energy and structure within the body'*.

Really?!

In an article for **Quack watch**, entitled "Questionable Organizations: An Overview", Stephen Barrett lists Zero Balancing Association as an organization which he views with *'considerable distrust'*. I don't blame him.

There are many other aberrations. Space limitations do not permit me to elaborate on them all. But I *have* to mention **absolute zero**! What balderdash! Zero **IS** absolute, my physicist friend! You don't say **sweet sugar**, do you?

1

I believe I was in grade three when, at the beginning of the school year, my mother told me that I should work hard and be number one in the class. I agreed. And I worked hard. When the rankings were out at the end of the year I found out that I was 27 and not one. I was elated. I could not wait until I told my mother the good news.

I was a happy customer when I wound my way home. A poet watching me would have said, "That boy has a lilt in his step."

But consider my chagrin when my mother, instead of being happy at my accomplishment, was quite angry. "Surely 27 is better than one," I bleated. "Yes, if you are talking about coconuts, and if you don't know what they are, there is one right on the top of your neck," my mother responded.

Rather brutal, I thought. Especially coming from one's mother!

It did not take very long to find out the uniqueness of being number one. The power of the number is awesome.

With its older brother zero, it controls computer language and systems – in other words, the entire world.

No other number has crept into the language and impacted our communication more. How many million parents have said, and how many million children have heard, "***Once*** upon a time..." I must say that I don't know the genesis of the word **once** in this context. Webster cleverly avoids any attempt at clarifying this. He simply says that it means, **at some definite time in the past** in addition to many other connotations like **one time and no more.** I also don't understand how this word can generate such immediacy by the mere addition of **at** as in **at once.** Nor do I understand the denotation of giving one the **once over.**

The word one, and thus the number, simply means a single unit or thing, though in an expression like **early one morning**, there is a sense of particularity. Wilfred Funk, the distinguished scholar and wordsmith traces the origin of the word one to the Latin **unus**, which has given rise to strong friendly words...**unity, unison, unanimous and union.**

The Latin word **integer**, which means a whole number in mathematics and thus **whole** or **in one piece**, yields us the word **integrity.**

Funk goes on to say that the word one gives us **atone**, because if we break up atone into two words, we get **at one.** When we have made atonement for a sin, we are **at one with God.**

Individuals and institutions strive to be the first, to be on top, to be the best – be it in sports, auto manufacturing or eating hotdogs. So we hear statements like, "So and so is the number one player in the world or such and such a bank has posted the most profit in a year." But many times, the occupants on the top are susceptible to falling off the perch. Take Roger Federer for instance – perhaps the best tennis player ever – who danced his way to the top while his opponents grunted, cussed, sweated and scrambled around on the court. He was on top for about 5 years when a matador called Nadal came from Spain and knocked him off. The victor would in turn be vanquished by a Serbian, but the matador would regain his top spot yet again. The spot on the top is ephemeral at best.

The word one has crept into colloquial use more than any other. When we immigrated to Canada from Uganda in 1965, we were bound for the Village of Boyle and *en route* we had stopped in Edmonton for a couple of nights. The hotel manager was rather curious about us because it was very evident that we were newcomers and when we declared that our destination was Boyle, he said, *"So, you are going to a one horse town, eh?"*

It would be many months before I understood the cultural impact of *eh?* No doubt you have read the book **Canajan, eh?** But I was mystified at the concept of having a single horse in a village. What would a single horse do in a town? I mean, why only one horse? Why not six or seventeen? I was too proud to ask but being a reasonably intelligent guy, I surmised that this equine specimen was fed and groomed and preserved for ceremonial occasions like leading a parade or something like that. Later on, I discovered that the village had no horse at all!

As I said, the word one has crept into idiomatic usage. We talk of **one-sided decisions, one-man committees**. We refer to people as **one-dimensional**. Several people are able to give the **one-two punch**. Not me!

I had better stop. I have to go to the hospital to see an old friend who went to a party a couple of days ago, had **one for the road** and on his way home wrapped his car around a tree. His superstructure is severely damaged.

2

I did not realize how important the number two is until I looked at myself in the mirror and said, "I could not have been here if two people had not got together and did their thing... unless I am an amoeba, which I am not." Noah knew this and he cleverly assembled his clients in pairs for his famous cruise.

Yes, it takes two to tangle, tango...

Mathematicians are always fond of pointing out the uniqueness of numbers and two *is* unique. This is the ONLY number that when added to itself or multiplied by itself produces the same result, i.e. 2+2=4; 2×2=4.

The dictionary defines the word (number) as **equivalent to the sum of one and one; one less than three.** But that is too simplistic. The connotations are vast and bewildering. With its cousins **second, double, di** and **bi** the number finds itself in a wide variety of uses, some of which are interesting, some uncomfortable, and some even offensive.

Second is the most interesting cousin because it is a real performer. It takes on many roles. One of the thespians in the galaxy of words!! (for the technically minded, the word could be a noun, verb or adjective).

Roberts, who wrote the definitive work on how to conduct meetings, says in his seminal book **Rules of Order** that in a meeting a motion made by someone will have to be **seconded** before a vote is taken. However chairmen are known to ignore this and go straight to the vote. I was once **seconded** for two years—('cond' is pronounced as 'fond') to another job while I was briefly working for the Auditor General's office in my home state.

But the most common use, in my opinion, is when the word is used as a unit of time equal to 1/60 of a minute known as a **second.** I have no clue, though, how it could relate to the numeral. It has just wormed its way into the usage! A **second** doesn't matter to me, but just ask Usain Bolt what he thinks about it.

I had mentioned that the number could be used in uncomfortable or offensive contexts. For instance, in spite of my vast experience in theatre, if anyone described me as a **two bit director,** I would be very offended. (Someone will have to explain why one quarter of a dollar is called **two bits.** I know there is some Spanish connection of some sort.)

Those who know me would agree that I always contribute my **two cents worth** at meetings, though I have a visceral dislike for meetings. But I am neither **two faced** nor **two fisted.** If you don't believe it, I care a **tuppence.** I characterize such critics as being **two dimensional** – lacking in depth of characterization.

Double is a cousin of two. With all its connotations, it is quite a versatile word. My brother-in-law was a **double agent**, now retired. He adopted a **double barrelled** name – Abbot-Brown. He is a huge fellow and looks very impressive in a **double breasted** suit. He has no compunction **double crossing** people.

I have a somewhat large business – easy ways to exterminate bed bugs. This venture involved a large investment, but I am able to keep track of my expenses and such using the **double entry** system of accounting. Being a cautious person, I always **double check** the entries. I don't want no problems with the tax guys. (oops, that is a **double negative!**)

A few weeks ago I attended a show at one of the theatres. It was advertised as a **double bill**—an orchestral concert in the first half, and a one act play in the second. The music was okay and the ensemble passable; but the **double bass** was not good at all. It was quite comical because the player was shorter than the instrument! I **doubled up** laughing.

I have always wondered why when two people sing or play the violin it is called a **duet**, but when you replace the instruments with rapiers it is called a **duel. Dual** is very different, of course. At one time I was a British citizen. But I gave it up when I became a Canadian citizen. I don't have **dual** citizenship and hence I cannot claim citizenship in two countries.

Di—not the late Princess Di—is another distant cousin. Rather a weakling because it cannot stand on its own. But in association with other morphemes, it takes on a new life. **Dichotomy**, for instance. But I will never understand why a person who speaks two languages is not called **dilingual.** No. It is **bilingual!** In fact, **bi** is more of a parasite than **di.** Many words have been invaded by this prefix – **bicarbonate, bilateral** to mention two. Oh, did you know that **biceps** means having two heads? I didn't. I thought it was just the name of a muscle in the forearm!

By the way English has 170 words with the prefix **di** and 210 words with the prefix **bi**! I counted.

The word **twin** is a vagrant who walked away. It has as much claim as **double.** We all know what a **twin born** is; also **twin beds.** But what about **twine?** This word originally meant **to encircle or enforce.** But today it means a string that has **two strands.** Certainly not what Rudyard Kipling meant when he said "East is east and West is west; but never the **twain** shall meet." **Twain** is only a spelling vagary.

Twin, twine, twain (an archaic form of two)—they are all the same; oh, **deuce** too.

3

When we talk of the number 3, we are dealing with the chief mystic number of all time. The figure 3 is important because it is made up of **1+1+1**. It is evenly balanced with a beginning, middle and an end, i.e., birth, living, and death. Three is emblematic of the Christian **Trinity**—the Father, Son, and Holy Ghost. But the importance of the number three is older than Christianity. Hindus talk about the **Trimurthi**, a **triad** of Hindu Gods—Brahma the Creator, Vishnu the Preserver, and Shiva the Destroyer. (**Tri** in Sanskrit means three.) In Classical mythology there is the **trio** of Graces, Fates, and Furies. Jupiter's lightning is **three forked** and Cerberus, the dog that guards the gates of Hades, has **three heads**.

With all these divine attributes, it was perhaps irresponsible to gift the Devil with a **Trident**! A bident or even a monodent (if I am using the correct words) would have been plenty for whatever use he put it to.

The most endearing concept of three is, perhaps, the oldest trinity known to man—father, mother and child. But then, we also have the 'threes' of earth, sea and the sky; of sun, moon and the stars. Sophocles talked about the libation of wine, honey and milk during religious practices. The Roman augurers were consulted three times. Multiples of three were much employed by witches in their incantations. The ultimate medico, Pliny, spat three times to make a dose of medicine effective. Jews pray three times a day. There are three wise monkeys. Remember the three wise men? Tom Sawyer and Huckleberry Finn, two of the earliest pharmaceutical researchers, did say that the important part of the 'spunk water cure' for warts was that the patient should turn around three times after dunking his hands.

Today most government bills need three readings before they get passed by the law-makers. If you play baseball, what do you have after three strikes?!

The other day someone told me, "You are sooo two dimensional." Well, I care **thruppence** for such criticism. My family is very critical of my sartorial habits. They complain that I compromise my gravitas by not wearing a **three piece** suit for formal functions. I don't, because if I did, I would look like a pocket edition of Sidney Longstreet or Orson Welles. The fact is that I can't breathe when I button down the waistcoat – vest, if you prefer.

But I can, thank God, rest on my laurels. I won the **triple** jump at the Inter- varsity games. I also won the **Triple Crown** in tennis–singles, doubles and mixed doubles. But I was rather below average during my student days. I never could master the **three R's**—reading, 'riting and 'rithmetic, which made me rank somewhere at the bottom of the class. I recall that I was ranked 27th when I was in grade three.

In my old age, among my many frailties, eyesight is a major issue. I have to wear **tri**focal lenses to navigate around the house. Messy affair, when you try to negotiate stairs, especially going down!! Once I tripped and while trying to hold on to the balustrade to avoid a major crash, I stretched my **tri**cep muscles. I believe it is a kind of extensor muscle along the back of the upper arm. I should ask Dr. Simon Cox. He knows a lot about such things.

By the way when Simon was a physician in Grande Prairie, (he has now emigrated to the Valhalla of retirees, Vancouver Island) he used to lead the Canada Day Parade riding a uni-cycle. He is over six feet tall and so it was quite a sight to see this man perched on top of the unicycle. I am glad he did not choose a **tri**cycle because he would have looked very silly. The tricycle is an aberration. It does not have the romance of the bicycle or the thrill of the unicycle.

A few years ago, I had to have a valve job done in my ticker. The surgeon said that my **tri**cuspid valve had to be replaced. I had always thought that 'cusp' meant either horn of the crescent moon. I also know that I have **tri**cuspid teeth. But a **tri**cuspid valve?? Beats me.

Anyway, the surgery was successful. I was happy when I was discharged early because I could convalesce in the comfort of my home. It is my routine to sit in front of the fireplace in the evening, sipping a **tri**ple sec. But the other day I noticed something that I had not paid attention to before. The embers were flying about because our fireplace screen is a **tri**ptych and hence not wide enough. I should invest in one with four panels.

Last week I got news that my favorite niece got **tri**plets. I was rather surprised though, because I could not imagine that wisp of a woman carrying three babies in her womb. Oh, well!!

I am getting ready for my annual summer trip to New York. This is when I recharge my batteries, as the vernacular goes. But while wandering around Times Square I have to be careful not to get sucked into playing **three card monte**.

Must run. The second part of a BBC **tri**logy called The **Tri**umvirate will begin in three minutes. But before that I must get my **three fingers of single malt** on the rocks, if I have run out of triple sec.

4

The number 4 was doing all right, holding its own, between its formidable neighbors 3 and 5, until a smart aleck literary aficionado coined the phrase '*four letter word*', specifically referring to vulgar, obscene words made of four letters. Since then, thousands of decent four letter words like love, milk, nose, spam etc., have retreated into the cavernous recesses of the dictionary, nervous about raising their heads.

This is a tragedy because, as I said, the number was holding its own. Abraham Lincoln, for instance, in his famous Gettysburg address took us back **four score and seven years.** He did not say three score and twenty seven years or five score minus thirteen years. Lord Macaulay reminded us that the British Empire spread to the four corners of the earth. Of course, he omitted to tell us how to find four corners on a globe! Possibly, he was inspired by compatriot John Dryden, who in his work Absalom and Achitopel wrote:

"When rattling bones together fly
From the four corners of the sky."

I am sure both these scholars believed that the earth was
flat and, perhaps, square! John Keats, on the other hand, tells
us that '**four seasons** fill the measure of the year.' He was,
obviously, not referring to Canada where we have only two
seasons: cold and not so cold.

The Bard made reference to this number too. In **Richard II**
he wrote:

"How long a time lies in one little word!
Four lagging winters and four wanton springs
End in a word: such is the breath of kings."

The good book talks about the four horsemen, the apoca-
lyptic vision, viz. **war, famine, pestilence and death,** personi-
fied as the major plagues of mankind. Whoever conceived
this could have said five horsemen and included politicians.
But he did not.

There are four directions – **north, south, east and west**.
North-northeast and south-southwest are aberrations, a foolish
attempt to confuse us. North by Northwest?! Pshaw. What
would a rotund man like Hitchcock know about these things?

Personally, I like the number. I like many things involving
the number. The **four poster bed**, for instance. But it must
have a canopy to catch the dust, and if in the tropics, lizards.

In 1965 when we moved from Uganda to Boyle, Alberta, I was quite surprised to see many tropical plants in people's houses – plants like hibiscus, geranium, petunia, nasturtium, and various species of the sunflower family. But I did not find the **four o' clock plant** (see picture below).

This native of Peru inexplicably opens and trumpets its flowers – yellow, violet, white, and variegated – around four in the afternoon.

It was while in Boyle that I was introduced to the **4-H movement**. The 4 H's are **Head, Hand, Heart and Health**. The movement is very strong in many rural parts of Canada.

The number four has great significance in all religions. The Hindus have four Vedas, a canonical collection of hymns, prayers and liturgical formulae that comprise the earliest sacred writings. In the Christian context, the major gospels came from four of Christ's disciples – Matthew, Mark, Luke and John. The four matriarchs of Judaism are Sarah, Rebekah, Leah and Rachel. Many religions believe in the four great elements – earth, water, fire, and wind.

A game of bridge requires four players, not three or five. Mammals have four legs, unlike the birds which seem to manage with two. Can you imagine how awkward it would be for an elephant if it had only two legs? The savannah would tremble if a herd of elephants hopped around like a troupe of kangaroos.

The human heart has four chambers. The hand has four fingers and a thumb. By the way, the fourth finger of the hand (the ring finger) is also moved when the little finger moves.

Quarter, a cousin of four, enjoys an unsullied reputation. A mundane meaning of the word would be 'one of four equal parts'. But it has a glamour far beyond that. The silver jubilee, for instance. Quarter of one hundred years of service, or a marriage! Closer to home we have a **quarter in coinage** (also called two bits), and a **quarter side of beef**. Farmland is measured in **quarters**, a quarter meaning an area that is quarter of a mile square. And farmers in olden days, before the invention of tractors used draught horses to do the grunt work. They preferred them to **quarter horses** that excel in speed, not especially suitable for farm work.

The most important person in the game of handball, a modern version of the Roman gladiator sport is the **quarterback**. I know, I know, it is called football and handball is an entirely different game. I am arguing that it cannot be called football (like soccer) because the feet are used only for running, and occasional kicking.

The **Barber Shop Quartet** has, of course, four singers. A symphony has four movements. Most string instruments have four strings.

Fourth is another cousin of four. It is the ordinal form of four. Its meaning is obvious, but the phrase **fourth estate** has specific connotations. It is a social or political force whose influence is not officially recognized. It most commonly refers to the news media, especially print journalism.

Americans celebrate Independence Day on the **4th of July** every year. And oh, I forgot; I am still searching for the **four leaf clover** because the common belief is that it bodes well for the person who spots one. As the name suggests it is a cluster of four leaves (normally the cluster has three leaves). Each leaf stands for something specific: the first is for faith, the second for hope, the third for love and the fourth for luck.

5

Five, of course, is half of ten or the sum of four and one. I suppose what crosses your mind when you think of five are the five senses or five fingers or, if you are a traveller, five star hotels. Historians among you would, I am sure, be reminded of the **five year plan**, a term for national economic development that originated with the first such plans adopted by the Soviet Union in 1928.

But if you are a golfer, you would think of the **five iron** used, I am told, in lofting the ball. This implement, once called a mashie, is something you can't buy in a **five and dime store**, which was an establishment which sold miscellaneous articles priced at five and ten cents. What **can** you buy these days with five or ten cents?!!

And you would think that five fingers refer to the digits of your hand. You would only be partially correct because there is a **plant** called **five fingers**, a native of New Zealand, belonging to the magnolia family.

When I moved to Canada from Africa, I had to go through a massive initiation process – naturally. So, among pastimes like curling, I was also introduced to a game called **five pins**. The object of the game, for the benefit of my readership in Chad, Nepal and similar far flung places, is to throw a ball down a highly polished lane of wood and to knock off five pins shaped like milk bottles. I could never master the technique. Always left a couple of pins unscathed.

The cousin of five, **fifth**, occupies a more exalted place in the life of Americans. It is the **Fifth Amendment**, an amendment to the constitution which guarantees the people due process of the law by providing a clause that no person shall be compelled in any criminal case to be a witness against himself. Neat, eh?!

But my own pleasant memories go to the months I spent in New York. Ah, **Fifth Avenue**!! What a place to shop: window shop, that is, except for the super-rich. Sacs, Tiffany's, Lord and Taylor, Bergdorf Goodman…I especially will never forget the occasion of my first visit to Fortunoff to look at a flatware set they had on sale for half the price – 250 dollars, 600 in today's dollar value. When I was leaving the store, a lady who seemed to be in a mighty hurry, bumped into me. She was dressed in a T-shirt, jeans and had a bandana covering her head. She said, "Sorry." The gravelly voice sounded familiar and I said, "Are you by any chance…?" Before I could finish the sentence she said, "Yes, I am. I am still sorry." She was actor Lauren Bacall!! Bacall was one of the sponsors of Fortunoff.

I would be loath to be branded a **fifth columnist** because temperamentally I would be useless as a spy or saboteur or propagandist. But I don't want to be a **fifth wheel** either; I do think that I am a useful human being, not a superfluous thing.

The number five has another cousin – one of Greek origin – a sneaky fellow who has great influence in our life – **penta**. Who has not heard of the **pentagon,** which, before it became the centre of power controlling the world, was just a geo-metrical figure with five sides, as opposed to, say, the triangle or the square!

I also think of the **pentameter**, especially the iambic variety, having struggled with it through college and during the productions of Shakespeare, reminding actors that it is as simple as de dum, de dum, de dum. But try to use that rhythm to recite, "To be or not to be…." See where you land!

I am always fascinated by track and field events in sports where people exhibit the results of their resolve and training to jump longer, run faster, vault higher and throw farther. To me the ultimate athlete is the decathlete who has to participate in 10 events – two times five. But please give some credit to the **pentathlete** who participates in five events – two sprints, two throws and one jump.

If you are the product of a similar educational system as mine, you would have used your fingers to count. Counting with fingers and toes is as old as mankind, I should think. Our decimal system is based on this and Roman numerals, unquestionably, were first represented human fingers. Note the linguistic hangover of all this in our mathematical word

digit from the Latin word *digitas,* meaning finger. In Papua New Guinea I noticed that many people use one hand for five, two for ten. 20 is the sum of the fingers and toes. Nothing after 20 counts!

6

In Shakespeare's play Richard II, York says, "But time will not permit: all is uneven, and everything is left at six and seven."

I am sure the Bard was referring to the popular English idiom **sixes and sevens** used to describe confusion and disarray.

And yet, in the galaxy of numbers, six occupies a unique position. It is a number of perfection. In the whole set from 0 to 10, six is the only number under ten that can be divided by 1, 2, and 3, called divisors. Six is also the only number that is both the sum (1+2+3) and the product (1x2x3) of three consecutive positive numbers.

Pythagoras the Greek mathematician called it "the scale of the world" because according to the Old Testament, Yahweh took **six days** to create the world. He also called it the "number of man" because he was created on the sixth day.

Staying with the religious theme, Christ had 6×2 apostles. Noah was 600 years old when the great flood occurred. The Star of David has six points.

It is not an accident that a day has six four-hour segments, an hour six ten minute segments and a minute six ten-second segments.

If you believe in polygamy, Henry VIII should be your reference point. He had six wives. Why he stopped at six, I am not sure.

Speaking of the Realm, once upon a time when their currency was pounds, shillings and pence, six penny meant, of course, **six pence**. However you cannot buy **six penny novels** for six pennies any more. Also the term **six penny nail** does not tell you its cost. It is actually a nail two inches long.

We all know what a **six-shooter** is. It used to be the most popular portable firearm that people carried. And who has not bought a **six-pack**! These became popular because it was easier on the elbow when you carted it around. And if you needed twelve you could buy two, instead of a case of 12 bottles… obviously heavier than cans.

In cricket, a game akin to baseball, if a player hits the ball and it flies over the boundary line, it is called a **sixer**. It is worth six runs, obviously.

The number six has two cousins – a Greek called **hexa** and a Latino called **sex(t)**. The most common word is **hexagon**, a figure that has six sides and six angles. I am sure you all have seen a bee hive.

Meanwhile **sex(t)** with 12 derivatives has also produced some interesting terms. The **sextant** is an instrument of navigation used in olden days to ascertain latitudes and longitudes. It got its name because its shape forms one sixth of a whole circle.

I suspect that for a pregnant woman, it is a heavy load to carry **sextuplets**. One baby is hard enough! The first set of sextuplets of whom all six survived are the Dilley sextuplets, shown below.

Before I **go six feet under**, (Why six? What is wrong with five?) I have to thank heaven for small mercies. I am not one of those with **hexadactyly.** If I did, I would have six fingers on each hand. It would have been a bummer in winter when I went shopping for gloves! I wonder if it is an advantage for piano players!

No better way to conclude this than talking about a famous street address in Brooklyn—**66 Water Street**. This is the home of Jacque Torre's Chocolate. Jacque, known as Mr. Chocolate, is a master pastry chef. Among the chocolate products he sells, the most popular is called Wicked Hot Chocolate featuring allspice, cinnamon and chili pepper.

7

In Shakespeare's comedy **Twelfth Night**, a distraught and love sick Orsino tells his court, "If music be the food of love, play on." He expected music to assuage his painful heart. Maybe music has that quality. But one thing is certain; I believe that most every human being loves/likes music. Those who don't, hopefully a minority, don't know what they are missing.

Music has a divine attribute as well, in the sense that our Gods are passionate (or at least partial) to music. Apollo was the Greek God of music, among other portfolios, and he played the lyre. Pan, a minor God of the wild, shepherds and such played the famous syrinx (Pan Flute). Minerva was the Roman Goddess of music. Hindus believed that Lord Krishna was a virtuoso flautist. Goddess Sarasvati played the veena.

But as far as the human voice is concerned, music in mundane, dry, technical terms is produced by the vibration of vocal folds (cords) in our throat in different ways. The western notations for the different kinds of vibrations produced, as every school boy knows, are: do, re, mi, fa, so, la and ti. Indian counterparts are sa, ri, ga, ma, pa, dha, and ni. So when you listen to a Pavarotti, Jessye Norman, Nat King Cole, Julie Andrews or Subbulakshmi sing, several different permutations and combinations of the vibrations (notes) come out to thrill us all.

Of course you have counted the notations and got the number 7.

In strictly arithmetical terms it is the number after six and before eight. I was alerted to the importance of the number seven when I was in grade school. One of the tasks was to memorize the **Seven Wonders of the World**. No one explained the significance of these wonders and in the absence of slide projectors, PowerPoints and such, conceptualizing them was also difficult, though I have a faint recollection of an equally faint picture of the Pyramids of Giza, which, incidentally, is the only one of the original seven wonders that has withstood the ravages of time.

But as time went by, a new set of 'seven wonders' was named – the Taj Mahal and the Great Wall of China being two of them.

Of all the numbers, seven has deep significance and was considered sacred by all the cultured nations of olden times.

The astronomical origin of this number is established beyond any doubt. "Man feeling himself at the mercy of the heavenly powers made earth subject to the heavens. The largest and brightest luminaries that he saw became the most important and powerful entities. They were the **seven planets**, ever remaining at an equal distance from each other and rotating in the same path. This suggested the eternal harmony of the universe."

So the number seven became sacred to him. The harmony of sound takes place on a smaller plain with the musical scale of the ever recurring seven notes. So it is not by accident that there are seven pipes in the **syrinx** of the aforementioned God Pan. Apollo's lyre had seven strings.

The Greeks had **seven sages**. In the middle ages an oath had to be taken before **seven witnesses**. Muslim pilgrims go around the Kaaba in Mecca **seven times**. The Menorah has **seven branches**.

The Hindus consider seven very important. The sacred books mention **seven sages** (sapta rishis), **seven worlds** (sapta lokas), **seven holy cities** (sapta puras), and **seven holy seas** (sapta samudras).

There are **seven days** in a week. Whether Saturday or Sunday is the seventh day varies across cultures. We all know that God rested on the seventh day. The rainbow has **seven colors**, and Snow White is accompanied by **seven dwarves**, not six or eight. Rome is built on **seven hills.**

September was the **seventh month** in the ancient Roman calendar (as the name suggests) but after the reform that led to the current order, the seventh month is July, a month named after the creator of the new calendar, Julius Caesar. He was born in July, 100 BCE.

Shakespeare divided the ages of man into seven. Why would Steven Covey pick seven in his famous book **The Seven**

Habits of Highly Effective People? And why would the code name of James Bond be **007**?

The deadly sins, also known as the cardinal sins are seven: **wrath, greed, sloth, pride, lust, envy, and gluttony.** In retrospect, I can truthfully say that I have committed only four of the above. Or is it five? I am not sure if I will ever reach **seventh heaven**.

As far as beverages go, I prefer **7UP** to ginger ale. **Seven up** is also the name of a game of cards (it is also called All Fours, Old Sludge or Pitch).

And, if you play craps, seven is the luckiest number.

Pythagoras called seven the perfect number: three plus four—the triangle and the square, the perfect figures.

8

When Jehovah asked Moses to lead the children of Israel to the Land of Canaan, he was traversing a terrain not especially well known for paved highways and sidewalks. Indeed, they did not even have a gravel path to walk on. In addition to the inhospitable terrain, there was an additional problem: snakes. So when Moses asked his boss to do something about it, He said, "Make a fiery serpent and set it on a pole; and it shall be that everyone who is bitten, when he looks at it, shall live." (Old Testament, Numbers 21.8.9).

In suggesting this, Jehovah must have taken inspiration from one of his minor colleagues of another era, Asclepius, the Greek god associated with medicine and health care. The Rod of Asclepius is, of course, a rod, entwined by a serpent. Later another Greek by the name of Hermes improved on it and designed a rod with two serpents and the product came to be known as the caduceus. After World War I, the caduceus was employed as an emblem by both the United States Army Medical Department and the Navy Hospital Corps. Even the American Medical Association used the symbol for a time, but in 1912 after considerable discussion, the caduceus was abandoned by the AMA and the Rod of Asclepius was adopted instead.

In mundane terms 8 is the number after 7 and before 9. But both numerically and figuratively, the number eight is associated with perfection. Like zero, it is fluent. In fact it does look like two zeros on top of each other. The fallen or lying down eight is used to represent infinity in mathematics.

Staying on the theme of mathematics, the number 8 is a power of two—two cubed—meaning 2 x 2 x 2 equals eight. And 2+2+2+2 equals eight. This is possible only with the number 8.

In spiritual terms eight is very important. The Buddhists believe in the **eightfold path** leading to the cessation of suffering and the achievement of self-awakening. Taoists believe in the **eight immortals** that are a source of inspiration.

Hanukkah is an eight-day Jewish holiday. Jesus Christ gave **eight beatitudes** in the Sermon on the Mount, recorded for all posterity in the Gospel of Matthew.

In Indian literary lore **ashtapathis** are Indian hymns in eight lines. The most famous of them all is called Gita Govindam symbolizing the eternal love of Lord Krishna for Radha.

But it is to the Chinese that the number has the greatest significance. Eight is considered the most fortuitous of numbers, making it the most coveted for addresses, phone numbers, number plates for vehicles, etc. Many try to get as many eights as they can in phone, fax and license numbers. I read somewhere that the Chinese Yellow Pages for the San Gabriel Valley in Los Angeles have more eight combinations than one thought imaginable (are there such things as Yellow Pages still available?!). California developer Raymond Chan's business phone number is 818 282 2828. In Hong Kong a personal license plate with the number eight can cost hundreds of thousands of dollars.

In the British system eight fluid **ounces** make a cup and eight **pints** make a gallon (surely, you Metrics out there have not forgotten the pint and the gallon). While on the British system, let me add that there are **eight furlongs** in a mile. A furlong has 220 yards, a yard has three feet and so on. I am sure 'furlong' is a strange word for many of you. In my school days, one of the permanent fixtures in an arithmetic test in the primary school used to be to reduce, say, 117 miles into furlongs, yards, feet and inches! The teachers when I went to school were a sadistic bunch!

Those in the United States army do not want to be discharged as per **Section 8** of the Military Code because that would mean that the officer is mentally unfit to serve.

Eight seems to be the culpable number behind the great tsunami of 2004 according to the leading astro-numerologist Sanjay Jumaani. The tsunami happened on December 26, and two plus six makes eight. Even the sum total of the numbers of the date on which the tsunami occurred – 26/12/2004 – is 17, and one plus seven make eight. According to him 8 is an unlucky number.

The close cousin of eight is '**octo**'. Thus the octopus has eight legs. (So does the spider.) An **octoroon** is a person who has one eighth black ancestry. And though the **octave** is universally recognized as a musical term, it also means an eighth part of a pipe of wine (a pipe is approximately 125 gallons).

9

Of all the single digit numbers, 9 is the most profound. It is the mathematician's delight. It is the logician's nightmare.

If the number one is divided by nine the result is 0.111111111... and if the number two is divided by nine, the result is 0.22222222... and if the number three is divided by nine the result is 0.3333333... and so on!

If you multiply 9 by any whole number (except zero) and repeatedly add the digits of the answer until it is one digit, you will end up with nine. A couple of examples: 2 X 9=18 (1+8=9); 578329 X 9=5204961(5+2+0+4+9+6+1= 27, and 2+7=9). There are several such examples of the magic of the number nine.

Superstition has it that a composer who writes the ninth symphony better not write another because he would be challenging fate. Beethoven, Mahler, Vaughn Williams, to name three, tinkered with the tenth and all of them died before finishing it. So if you have finished composing nine symphonies, engage yourselves in something else like garment design, horticulture or philately.

The number nine has a very important place in mythology. Many years ago when my daughter and I were in Iceland, we learnt that Norse mythology recognized nine realms of existence. Eight of the realms were embodiments of opposites: **fire and ice, heaven and hell, creation and destruction, light and darkness.** These realms converged on the **centre realm**, where humans lived out their lives.

In Greek mythology, **nine goddesses** called the **Muses** were responsible for inspiring musicians, artists and writers. One recalls that our beloved Bard sought the assistance of the Muses before beginning the epic adventure in Henry V. "O, for a Muse of fire...." he said.

According to one of the famous legends in Celtic mythology there were **nine magical hazel trees** at the centre of the Otherworld. They hung over the Well of Wisdom and dropped their fruits into the well, thus imparting wisdom and inspiration to all who drank the water from the well.

In astrology, the **ninth sign** of the zodiac is Sagittarius, identified by the Greeks as the Centaur. Centaurs were magical creatures known for their skills as archers, philosophers and predictors of the future.

Christ died at the **ninth hour** and the incantations of the witches who destroyed Macbeth were, "Thrice to thine, and thrice to mine, and thrice again to make nine."

In **The Divine Comedy** Dante suggests that there are **nine circles of Hell** and **nine spheres of Heaven**. In the Middle Ages nine was considered, first and foremost, the angelic number.

In Tolkien's **The Lord of the Rings**, there were nine Nazguls – nine men who succumbed to Sauron's power and attained near immortality as wraiths.

In French the word '**neuf**' means both 'nine' and 'new'. In German the words for nine and new are '**neun**' and '**neu**'. In Spanish they are '**nueve**' and '**neuvo**'. As you count and reach nine, you know you are about to make a **new** start.

The word (number) has crept into idiomatic and figurative English and proverbs. If I get a new start in life (rather unlikely at this stage of the game) I will be **on cloud nine** – euphoric. The cat has **nine lives** as we all know. **And a stitch in time saves nine**, not eight or ten. Time was when people thought that I was a snob having always appeared **dressed to the nines**. But I let those comments pass me like the idle wind. We always want to **go the whole nine yards** and not leave things half done. Many people hold **nine to five jobs** even though they might actually report for work at half past eight or leave work at seven.

Only about **one ninth** of the mass of an iceberg is visible above water. Apparently something the crew of the Titanic gave scant attention to.

There are **nine judges** on the Supreme Court. Nine is a priceless aid to retailers who can play on the psychology of the customer and sell things for $4.99 and $ 99.99 – not quite $5 nor $100.

Redivider is a word with nine letters and is also the longest palindrome in the English language. (A palindromic word has the same sequence of letters backwards or forwards.) **Madam** is another example. An article on palindromes appears elsewhere in this book.

10

According to Hindu cosmology, life in this universe is created and destroyed once every 4.1 to 8.2 billion years, which is the end of a period called Yuga. It is one full day and night for Brahma, the creator.

The life of the universe goes through ten Yugas, Brahma appears in ten incarnations or avatars in each one of them, the last being **Kali Yuga.** During this period the universe is totally destroyed and is reborn.

We are in the Kali Yuga now, and proof of this is plenty if we look at what is happening around us. Havoc is caused by climate change. Of course, many Republican lawmakers in the United States believe that it is a hoax, even though the Pontiff reminded everyone that climate change is real, that humans are responsible for the damages and that we have a responsibility to take care of all living things. Sectarian violence is killing millions of people everywhere in the world, terrorists of various shades are having a heyday and the Soviet era is poised to make a comeback. Child mortality is increasing in the world. Iran or North Korea could start a nuclear war.

All of these telltale signs indicate that Kali Yuga is right here.

I am writing all this because Kali Yuga is presided over by Kalki, the tenth incarnation of God (according to the Hindus) and thus a very important number in the grand scheme of things.

In Hindu mythology Ravana, the King of Sri Lanka, abducted Sita the wife of Lord Rama. Ravana had ten heads. In all pictorial depictions of this monarch, the face is clean shaven, except for a handle bar moustache. One would think that shaving ten faces might have been a bit of an issue, but then he had twenty arms. Easy!

The number ten is important in other religions as well. **The Ten Commandments** of Exodus and Deuteronomy are considered the corner stones of Judaism and Christianity. Jews observe the annual **Ten Days of Repentance** beginning with Rosh Hashanah and ending with Yom Kippur.

The **decimal** is a term relating to or denoting a system of numbers based on the number ten.

In English **decimal** means tenth, **decimate** means reduce by a tenth and **denary** means the unit of ten. The Roman numeral for five is, of course **V** and ten being made of two fives, it is represented by two V's one on top of the other, the narrow points touching – X.

Many ancient cultures calculated with numerals based on ten. In fact, the ingenious method of expressing every possible number using a set of ten symbols originated in India. In Sanskrit the term for ten is **das.**

We have ten digits in each hand, and children everywhere have used them to help compute.

Number 10 Downing Street is one of the famous mailing addresses in the world.

In Texas people wear the **ten gallon hat;** and a **ten foot pole** is something that you wouldn't touch something with. If you are in the army **ten-four** means 'message understood'. We all know that genius is ten percent inspiration and ninety percent perspiration. This is true **nine times out of ten,** not seven times out of eight.

In the Olympics the person who wins the **decathlon** is considered the best athlete in the world because he has to compete in ten events and perform well. In boxing if by the count of ten the floored boxer is not on his feet, he is declared a loser. It is also the highest score possible in Olympics gymnastics competitions.

Art

ART

The aim of art is to represent not the outward appearance of things, but their inward significance - **ARISTOTLE**

Art in its broadest manifestation makes one's life worthwhile and in many cases serves as a release valve when pent-up emotions have a stranglehold on the human condition. Art is twice blessed, to borrow an expression from the Bard. It provides an outlet for the individual who is eager to release his creative urges. It also provides a vicarious pleasure to those who are seeking a brief relief from the vicissitudes of life.

For purposes of this section of the book, I am taking a broad interpretation of the word and hence I have included all forms of visual and performing arts. Some of the articles reflect a certain levity and self-deprecating humor, but art has been a discipline that I have always taken seriously. Except drama I have not seriously studied or participated in any of the other forms, but even at an early age I had been exposed to all forms, and my parents had tried to inculcate in me a sense of appreciation for it all.

Having had the good fortune to visit most of the major museums in the world, having had the opportunity of listening to many iconic performers of music, having watched the performance of top notch dancers and actors, I feel contented in the thought that life has been extremely generous in giving me the opportunity to appreciate art vicariously.

SUPREMATISM

I do have many failings in my intellectual makeup – chinks in the armor, as it were. For instance, I cannot appreciate art–as in paintings, sculptures etc. Rather, the meaning or significance of many products that are touted as art eludes me. The family waxes eloquent about it. The wife and daughter rave about Group of Seven, Frida and Diego and such people. The son gushes about the fact that he has seen **Guernica** in the Museo Reina Sofia in Madrid.

Me? Nada.

Now. I do *understand* da Vinci's **Mona Lisa** or Vermeer's **Girl with a Pearl Earring**. Even when I see Turner's **Fishing Boats in a Sea Breeze**, I can understand it – sort of. But when I look at **Three Musicians** by Picasso ($21 million, if you please!), I am hard pressed to recognize any human beings at all in the painting. When I see Henry Moore's two huge, misshapen chunks of bronze, if I am supposed to believe that they are actually two reclining figures, I raise my eyebrows. Or when I see Ai Weiwei produce a pile of 100 million porcelain pieces shaped like sunflower seeds, each individually hand painted, the total weighing 150 metric tons, and I am asked to believe that it is "his commentary on mass consumption, Chinese industry, famine and collective work" I just give up.

What has this to do with Suprematism, you ask. Well, to answer that I have to go back in time. To 1967, in fact. That year we went to Montreal to see Expo '67. The most talked about pavilion was Buckminster Fuller's geodesic dome. There were many exhibits inside the dome, the most important one being the Apollo space capsule. Many paintings by contemporary American artists were also exhibited. One of them was a large canvas, 5.4m X 2.4m. It had two vertical stripes of dark blue on either side of another stripe of red. I am not sure if many noticed it. I did not. But it stormed into public attention when, in 1990, the National Gallery of Canada purchased it for 1.8 million dollars. All of a sudden the artist, Barnett Newman, became rich and famous. The painting is called **Voice of Fire**. When I heard the news, I told myself that I could do something like that! But someone beat me to it. John Czupryniak, who owned a nursery in Montreal promptly went to the hardware store, bought three pieces of plywood, two cans of paint, replicated **Voice** and stuck in on the front lawn of his house. When there was huge public outcry about the purchase, the curator said, "You have to look at your understanding of the metaphysical dimension of life."

Really??!!

Still, the desire to create something along the lines of **Voice** stayed with me, and was suddenly rekindled when I was in St. Petersburg. I was doing the obligatory tour of Hermitage. There was a large crowd in one of the rooms and I was told that it was a retrospective of a Russian painter called Kazimir Malevich. He had many monochromatic paintings on display. Various geometrical shapes in different colors. One of them was called **White on White.** You were supposed to see a white square on a white canvas. People were gawking at it. I admit I only saw a white canvas. But I got the idea. When I returned, I went to the local hardware store and bought the necessary supplies and came up with a masterpiece— even if I say so (see below).

As you can see, it is green and if you look carefully, you will see green lines. I did find it difficult to give it a suitable title. **Green on Green** would not be original. So I called it **Untitled**. Many famous painters have done it in the past. When they themselves have no clue about what the heck they have painted, they call it "Untitled".

Years from now, some curator in some museum would defend the spending of millions on my painting and explain that it is "an eloquent and compelling study of the existential threat to man's affectionate attachment to green and thus his relationship with nature"!

So, back to Suprematism. "It is art based on the supremacy of pure artistic feeling rather than visual depiction of objects." It was a movement originally started by Kazimir Malevich in 1915. You don't worry about form, texture, perspective and such. All you need is a surface. And some paint.

DANCE—THE PASTIME
OF THE GODS

For my post graduate work in theatre at New York University, I had elected to pursue a somewhat eclectic field called Performance Studies. Among the various aspects of the subject, one that I enjoyed most was rituals around the world, and their relation to theatre. To help us, our professor who was well known for conceptualizing Performance Theory, brought to the class iconic practitioners like Peter Brook, Victor Turner and Alvin Ailey, to name three.

The Alvin Ailey Dance Company in New York was already famous, especially with the premiere of ***Revelations*** in 1960. The production in three parts celebrates the uniqueness of African-American experience and the preservation/enrichment of the American modern dance heritage. Using spirituals, songs, sermons, and the blues, ***Revelations*** explores the places of deepest grief and holiest joy in the soul.

I believe Ailey was around fifty when he and a few of his star pupils spent half a day with us. Among other things, he touched upon Hindu mythology and how dance is deeply and inextricably intertwined with religious concepts. In an unforgettable moment, Ailey demonstrated the classic pose of Lord Shiva (Nataraja). I was the only Indian in the group and I was astonished to see this black man posing exactly like the bronze statue that millions have seen around the world (see below).

Nataraja is the supreme lord of dance in the Hindu pantheon and his signature piece called the **Thandava** symbolises the cosmic cycles of creation and destruction as well as the daily rhythms of birth and death. The illustrated pose is a marvellously unified and dynamic composition expressing the rhythm and harmony of life. It always reminds me of Leonardo da Vinci's **The Vitruvian Man**!

The Greeks believed that dance was the pastime of the Gods. This might be because the ordinary Greek was not, perhaps, nimble of foot (he preferred fighting and building wooden horses).

One wonders why the mortals have left a perfectly normal motor activity to the Gods. Nietzsche said that he would believe only in a God that knew how to dance! Centuries before that, Hindus already had conceived Nataraja. Ame-No-Ume (the goddess of dawn, mirth and revelry in the Shinto religion of Japan) brought forth the sun by dancing. Apollo was a superb dancer and Dante pictured Christ at the centre of the circling dancers of heaven.

But dance is not an everyday language, although the material is movement that man avails himself of in his everyday life. And when we watch mere mortals who can transform muscular movements into something breathtaking and artistic, we want to concede that it is, indeed, a pastime of the Gods. And that Fred Astaire, Gene Kelly, Martha Graham, Donald O'Connor, Gregory Hines, and Alvin Ailey were blessed.

Revelations has been performed many times around the globe, transcending barriers of faith and nationality and appealing to universal emotions. It has been performed in over 70 countries and an estimated 25 million people have seen it. Perhaps it was not strange that the company decided to reprise the show at the New York City Centre on New Year's Eve in 2013.

But what was really strange is nothing short of astonishing. Mazazumi Chaya, the associate artistic director of Alvin Ailey American Dance Theatre, had an idea: why not ask some of the stars of the original production to participate? Thus it was that Elizabeth Roxas-Dobrish (age 55), Linda Denise Fisher-Harrell (age 43), and Donna Wood Sanders (age 59) got a call from Chaya.

Really?! Is it not like trying to get Sean Connery (87) to play James Bond again? Of course, at first, they thought it was a big joke. Soon they realized that it was not; Chaya was dead serious.

They got an offer they could not refuse. Elizabeth had had two hip replacements in the last four years. But she got to work. She hired a physio therapist, an acupuncturist; she took a good look at her diet and started attending classes again. She knew that she couldn't perform the same way she did when she was young. In an interview she said, "When you are younger, you have everything—you have the flexibility, you have no fear. But you don't savor every step, every movement of every fingertip, and every beat of the music. I feel like I'm tasting food for the first time."

Sarah Lyall wrote in the New York Times, "The other day at the rehearsals, the petite Roxas-Dobrish danced with her partner—Jamar Roberts, 31—for the first time. The *Fix Me Jesus* portion (see next page) is intimate and gruelling, requiring the woman to push her body to extremes and put absolute trust in her partner.

Elizabeth Roxas-Dobrish, 55, a former member of the Ailey Company, rehearsing "Revelations" with Jamar Roberts, a current dancer. (Andrea Mohin/The New York Times)

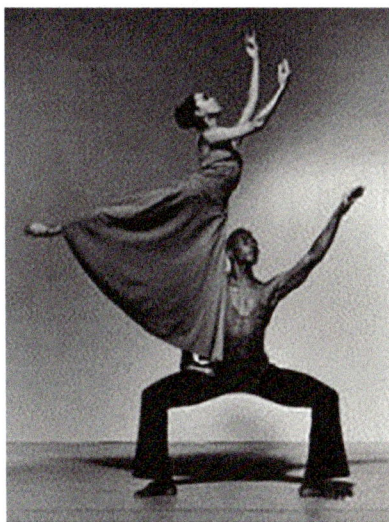

Elizabeth Roxas-Dobrish with Andre Tyson in "Revelations" during her years with Alvin Ailey American Dance Theater (Jack Mitchell photo)

Afterwards she said she felt an immediate connection – the dance kind of flowed; but she worried that Roberts would feel that he was dancing with his grandmother.

Roberts said, "Not at all. I felt that I needed to be delicate, not because she is old, but because she really is a jewel. She is legendary. I didn't want to do anything or say anything that would make it a bad experience for her."

P.S. I have found a five minute video of *Fix Me Jesus*. Do take time to watch this exquisite piece of work. The site is given below.

http://www.youtube.com/watch?v=4CXk1mQVCgI

CULINARY ART

In 1966 my colleagues in Boyle School, Alberta (where I was the principal) and I had to go to Edmonton for the annual convention of the Alberta Teachers Association. This was my first trip to the metropolis since my arrival in the country a few months before. On the second day of the convention, one of the group suggested that we go 'smorgasbord' for lunch. I assumed that it was the name of a restaurant. When we walked in, the layout struck me as strange and even after we sat down nobody appeared with a printed menu. Someone came to take the orders for beverages and that was that. I did notice a couple of long tables with a glass roof over them and assorted food was kept in steaming containers. I was anxious not to display my ignorance and so I sat at the table waiting for something to happen. Then one of them said, 'let us go' and then I realized that it was up to us to go the table and help ourselves to whatever we wanted to eat. And however much we wanted too!

Later I learnt that 'smorgasbord' is a Scandinavian term meaning that food is served on a buffet or cabinet and you help yourself to the fare. It is a bewildering experience the first time you try it.

Smorgasbord became internationally known at the 1939 New York World's Fair when it was offered at the Swedish pavilion's Three Crowns Restaurant. The table, in addition to food, had floral arrangements.

Decorating the food and the plate in which it is served is generally a western concept. In fact in culinary schools how you present the food is paid a lot of attention. So much so that sometimes when a dish is served, you feel reluctant to touch it lest you disturb an artistic creation. This is more evident in buffet style service where the artists (yes, culinary artists) display their skill to such an extent that it would appear to be a travesty to disturb a beautifully laid out table. Look at the two examples that follow and you will get my drift. But you are in an eatery and not a museum and so you reluctantly deface the plates and dig into the food!

In good restaurants your *entrée* is also served with some kind of decoration–a sprig of parsley or carrot julienne artistically placed, a radish shaped like a flower, or tendrils drawn with sauce on the plate, so that you look at it for a while before putting your knife to it. But that, of course, does not guarantee that the food is equally exciting. It could even be a ruse to take your mind away from the quality (or lack thereof) of the food that you are about to consume! I recall going to Maxim's—yes, THE Maxim's of Paris—and ordering *Sole meunière* and realizing that the fish was uncooked inside!! And it is a well-known fact that you DO NOT send the food back, because you have no idea what an offended chef would do to get even with you. Spitting in it is a common form of retaliation, I am told. Perhaps one is better off settling for Kung Pao chicken served on a lukewarm plate in a Chinatown restaurant than for braised chicken, however embellished ,served in Noma restaurant in Copenhagen.

But what lengths will a culinary artist go to in order to present you with something as ordinary as a cup of coffee? A cup of latte, for instance?

Basically latte means coffee with steamed milk. But 'latte art' is the latest rage in Japan. Look at this spectacular latte shown below and tell me if you ever will have the heart to drink the product that is in the cup.

It is, indeed, a shame that one has to drink the 'art work' only to evacuate it later in the form of malodorous you-know-what.

DOES SAD MUSIC MAKE US HAPPY?

In 1972, Art Ross, a member of the English faculty of the College in which I was working, chose to move out of the province, and while downsizing prior to his departure he sold me his turntable and record collection. I still have some of the records – now collectors' items. One of them was a performance by a musician named Michel Rubin, an American who is considered one of the greatest violinists of the twentieth century. He died in 1971 at the age of 35, and as such the release was hardly a year old. One of the tracks on the LP was a short piece called **Meditation: from Thaïs**. It is written for solo violin and orchestra.

I have to admit that I had never heard such a sad piece of music in my life.

The **Meditation** is a symphonic *entr'acte* performed between the scenes of Act II in the opera **Thaïs** written by French composer Jules Massenet, and the piece is approximately five minutes long. The story is about Athanaël, a Cenobite monk, who confronts Thais, a beautiful, Hedonistic courtesan and devotee of Venus. Athanael attempts to persuade her to leave her life of luxury and pleasure and find salvation through God. It is the time of reflection following the encounter that **Meditation** is played. The choice for Thaïs is painful because she is in love with the monk.

I have brought this up because quite recently I happened to read results of independent research studies done in Tokyo that posit that sad music makes a person happy. Kazuma Mori and Makota Iwanga of the Hiroshima University in Japan, who have published the results of their research in **Frontiers in Psychology**, claim that perceiving sadness in music can actually induce pleasant feelings in the listener.

The feelings evoked by works of art aren't direct, real world emotions but aesthetic ones. There is a difference between emotions perceived and those actually felt. In other words the listener does not actually experience the conflict going through the mind of Thaïs and instead "enjoys" it vicariously. We all feel "good" watching a sad movie, reading a sad novel because we are in a safe place while indulging in the emotion.

In a study at the universities of Kent in England and Limerick in Ireland, done approximately at the same time, researchers found pretty much the same thing as their Japanese counterparts. Their findings were published in the journal **Psychology of Music**. According to them one motive for listening to sad songs is that the music is being perceived as "beautiful". Researchers found that the "beautiful" music offered a direct correlation to mood enhancement.

Music generally impacts our emotional state, which is why it is extensively used by therapists to help clients improve their health in several domains, such as cognitive functioning, emotional development, and social skills. "Moving to music" is a very popular component in the therapy protocol. I have used music extensively in drama to help develop character and portray emotions.

I am not very familiar with the whole repertoire of western music and so I was curious to find if there are many other pieces like **Meditation.** I found several. I mention one in particular: Schubert's String Quintet in C. It is "lyrical, plaintive, nostalgic…" The circumstances under which he wrote the piece are also interesting and important. His health was sinking, and the piece which possesses 'bottomless pathos' reflects the pain and the mental turbulence he was going through. He did not live to hear the piece performed. He died when he was only 31.

However, among the 10 best classical 'tear jerkers', I prefer Samuel Barber's Adagio for Strings. One critic wrote, "It is full of pathos and cathartic passion, it rarely leaves a dry eye."

I am sure many of you have heard **Meditation** at one time or another. However, I am strongly suggesting that you listen to (and watch) the performance of Hungarian musician Katica Illenyi. You could not be blamed if you thought that Katica was actually playing the role of Thaïs while playing the violin. For your convenience I am providing you with the link.

https://www.youtube.com/watch?v=RZHIAbI9opg

Coming back to the question raised by the title. I believe that the terms 'sad' and 'happy' need to be clarified. People who watch operas and Bollywood movies would have noticed how the hero or heroine bursts into song while portraying an agonizing scene. While the character is in pain, the audience is not. The listener is just sympathizing, feeling it vicariously through the artist's experience. Though we might tear up and reach for Kleenex, we are not 'hurt' as the character is. In The Sound of Music when Maria sings "These are a few of my favorite things", the song leaves us in a 'happy' state even though our own list of favorite things might be different.

MONA LISA WAS A MOM

And at last it can be told.

Mona Lisa was a mom.

The enigma that has been confounding artists and art lovers for the last 500 years has been explained. Nat King Cole's question, "Is it your way to hide a broken heart?" has been answered. Mona Lisa was pregnant or had just given birth to a baby. More likely the latter, because the smile may have expressed the weary joy of a mother with a newborn.

This is, of course, if you believe a team from the National Research Council of Canada. Using infrared technology that allowed them to see beneath the layer of varnish, the researchers John Taylor and Francois Blais found that Leonardo da Vinci's model had a gauzy layer over her head dress they say was typically worn by pregnant women of the time or mothers who had recently given birth. The filmy robe was called a *guarnello.*

The description of the smile has become a cliché – the enigmatic smile – though Nat King Cole preferred to use the term 'mystic smile'. Dozens of theories have been put forward to explain it – from the ridiculous to the sublime. The issue of pregnancy was, indeed, raised once, but it was laughed at. Others suggested that she smiled the way she did because she had lost her two front teeth!

The findings announced at a press conference in Ottawa on the 26th of September 2015 could well have changed the way both experts and millions of tourists see the painting when they visit the Louvre.

Taylor and Blais used their scanner to determine that the poplar panel on which the painting was done is in good shape and is at no risk of degrading under its current storage conditions. The scan used a resolution ten times finer than the human hair! The panel has a 12 cm split or crack on the top but this dates back to the 18th or 19th century.

The researchers also confirmed what art experts have been wondering about the technique da Vinci used in painting the masterpiece. It is called *sfumato* or smoky – a technique that continues to elude experts. Taylor said, "It is extremely thinly painted and extremely flat and yet the details of the curls of the hair, for example, are extremely distinct. So the technique is unlike anything we have ever seen before."

For the source of the title, one has to go to the biography of da Vinci published 30 years after the death of the artist and inventor. The author Giorgio Vasari identified the sitter as Lisa Gherardini, the wife of a wealthy silk merchant from Florence. "Mona" is a common Italian contraction of "madonna" meaning 'my lady', the equivalent of the English 'madam'. So the title means Madam Lisa. In modern Italian the short form of 'madonna' is usually spelled 'monna'.

The Mona Lisa has acquired an iconic cult status in popular culture. Andy Warhol consecrated her as a modern icon, similar to Marilyn Monroe or Elvis Presley. As a cult painting, it has been the subject of many references in popular culture and *avant garde* art. More than a dozen songs have been renditioned by well-known artists including Willie Nelson, Elton John, Bob Dylan, and, of course, Nat King Cole. The painting has also inspired many movies, at least 16, as far as I know. And then there is the **Da Vinci Code**.

The painting was stolen in 1911, and in 1956 it was severely damaged when someone doused it with acid. A few months later a fellow from Bolivia threw a rock at it. The painting is now encased in bulletproof security glass.

Mona Lisa belongs to the French government, and used to occasionally go on tour. From December 14, 1962 to March 1963, the government lent it to the United States to be displayed in New York and Washington. In 1974 it was exhibited in Tokyo and Moscow.

But there will be no more tours. It is permanently enclosed in a climate controlled glass cage. It is too expensive to move, anyway. The insurance on it is in excess of 645 million dollars!!

Compared with some of the other invaluable masterpieces, Mona Lisa is quite small. It measures 30" x 20".

Not quite relevant to the article: In the original, Mona Lisa has her right hand over the left. But I do recall seeing a photograph of a painting with her left hand over the right.

Oh, by the way, did you know that the painting does not show any facial hair – neither eyebrows nor eyelashes?

ARE WE SUPPOSED TO "UNDERSTAND" ART?

In her scintillating play **Art**, French playwright Yasmina Raza indirectly asks the question 'what constitutes art'. The story is about Serge, a dermatologist in Paris who purchases a painting for 200,000 francs—something he cannot really afford. It is a canvas which is white and "if you look carefully you will see white lines." One of his friends, Marc, is outraged that he would waste money on what he considers is a piece of s!#t and asks another friend Yvan to go and have a look. Which he does. When they meet again Marc asks Yvan his opinion and further poses the question, "Were you moved by the painting?"

The technique of monotone paintings has been addressed in one of my previous articles. (Suprematism, page 93) Does a white canvas qualify as art, and is art supposed to "move" the viewer? In other words does a work of art evoke any emotional stirrings?

A response or reaction to a work of art is surely a personal thing. Do Picasso's **Dora Maar** and Vermeer's **Girl With the Pearl Earring** "affect" us in the same manner? Do we "like" one more than the other? Given an option to buy, which one would be the obvious choice? And why?

Sometimes it is difficult to understand what the work means or stands for. Henry Moore's sculptures are a case in point. His work **Two-Piece Reclining Figure** to me looks like a chunk of misshapen bronze. Ai Weiwei almost filled the Turbine Hall of Tate's Museum in London with **Sunflower Seeds**—100 million of them. 150 tons of them. Each one was carved in porcelain and hand painted to look like sunflower seeds. They were supposed to "allude to the globalization and mass production in China that caters to Western consumerism and to the deemed, insignificant element at the bottom of the production chain—thousands of cheap labors, assembly lines in gigantic factories and tedious procedures". How many of the millions of people who have seen this actually got it? If not, does it matter? More than likely, many people would have reflected on the monstrous amount of effort put out by 1,500 artisans who painstakingly painted each seed by hand.

Or do we better appreciate sculptures like Michelangelo's **David** because we "understand' the work?

Do we have to "understand" a work of art when we go to an art gallery? If one is not an aficionado of art, what would Chagall's **Green Violinist** mean? If we don't understand the pieces, why go to the gallery at all? Which raises the question what is the purpose of art?

I don't have the answers, but two philosophers Alan de Botten (England) and John Armstrong (Australia) seem to. In the bestselling book **Art As Therapy**, these two scholars propose a new way of looking at familiar masterpieces and art in general. They suggest that art can be useful, relevant and above all else therapeutic for their viewers. The book, which is variously described as "engaging", "lively", "controversial", is packed with 150 examples of outstanding art, architecture and design, while chapters on politics, sex, love, nature, and money show how art can help with many common difficulties – from forging relationships and finding happiness to accepting mortality. The authors claim, "Seeking to help readers develop a deeper understanding of art and of themselves in equal measure, the book provides fascinating reading for those familiar with art as well as those new to the subject."

But they did more than just write the book. They decided to curate an exhibition that brings the ideas of the book to life. They picked three museums – the Rijksmuseum in Amsterdam, The Art Gallery of Ontario in Canada and the National Gallery of Victoria in Melbourne. The curators picked select works from the museum collections and organized them under the five workaday rubrics like politics, sex, etc. For each piece of art, the curators wrote a problem and then suggested aspects of the work that might help solve that problem. Armstrong hastened to add, "What we have written up is not trying to explain the truth about the work. It is not saying, this is what you should think. It is us saying, "That is our comment: now what is yours?"

Murray Whyte of the Toronto Star is one critic who didn't particularly applaud the work of the two scholars. In his opinion the whole exercise ignored the colossal, towering question of why on earth, in our chockfull lives of forced utility, we can't have one single thing that is mysterious, enigmatic and does not particularly stand for anything.

I tend to agree.

As a postscript, I thought Oscar Wilde's take on art is appropriate in this context. Through Dorian Gray he says, "All art is useless, because its aim is simply to create a mood. It is not meant to instruct or to influence action in any way. It is superbly sterile..."

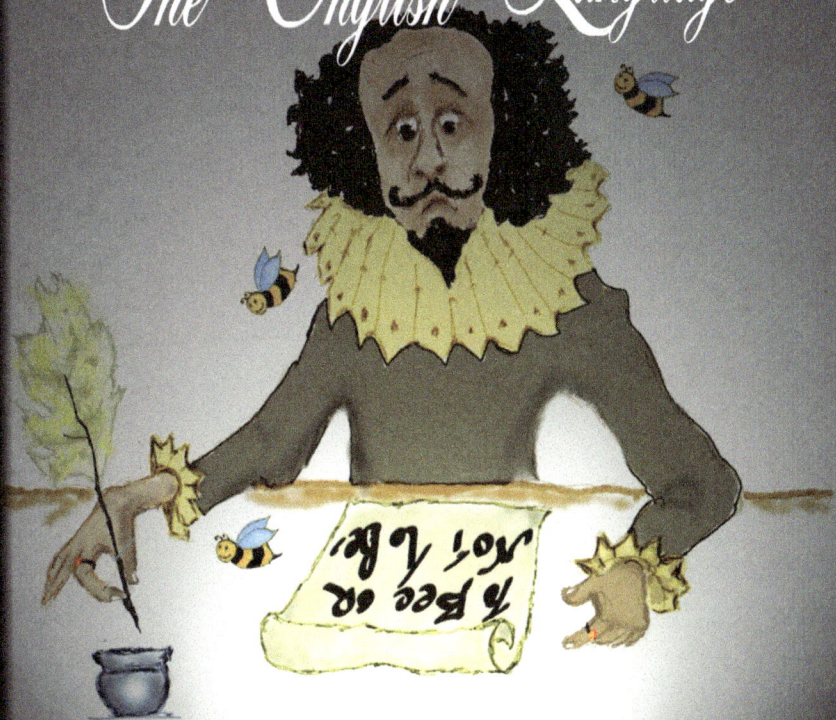

THE ENGLISH LANGUAGE

English is spoken by many people in many countries and it is the third most commonly spoken language in the world. Chinese and Spanish occupy the top two spots.

Hundreds of thousands of people have written their take on the English language and hence the question arises: what more is there to talk about?

Language impacts different people differently. For a person very passionate about the romance of words, language offers new vistas, nuances and excitement. It is the same old thing seen in a different light. A language grows by the addition of new words and expressions and I am astonished at the rate at which English has grown. Some of the articles in this section will address that.

I have also included examples of where people who are not quite in control make bloopers that are hilarious. Mrs. Malaprop was a fictitious character created by Sheridan in his play Rivals. But the 43rd President of the United States freely indulged in producing malapropisms.

This section is again written in a breezy style, but you're not surprised by that, are you?

GETTING THE HANG OF IT

Like many others, I like to read myself to sleep. Not Proust or Frye, mind you, but something less cerebral – say, John Grisham or Jeffrey Archer. Thus, the other night, I was reading '**Swimming to Catalina**' by Stuart Woods, and came across the following passage. "*Ciano produced his own cellular phone, called his assistant and ordered preparations for the test. He hung up. 'Welcome to Hollywood,' he said, grinning.*"

Normally I would have gone on reading. But something stopped me, and I had to ask myself, how does one hang up a cellular phone? This led on to other questions, and ended up examining the use of the word 'hang'.

Well, **hang**, *per se* is a harmless word. It only means "*fasten from some elevated point without support from below*", says the dictionary. A more technical definition suggests, "*to fasten so as to allow free motion within given limits upon a point of suspension*". Both the definitions make sense to me, especially when you **hang** a person. There should be no support from below and for those who seek black comedy, the subject of the hanging—in this case a rustler, shall we say—will move freely within given limits, i.e. once you whip the horse away.

But you can **hang** a door with less traumatic results or adjust the hem (of a skirt) so that it will **hang** evenly and at a proper height. You can **hang** buntings and flags. You can fasten something to a wall, as in **hanging** wall paper. You can, of course, also **hang** a picture. However, to hang wall paper you would be well advised not to use nails.

The other day, when my wife admonished me for not hanging the masks we had collected from around the world, I had no recourse but to **hang my head** in shame. They had been languishing in a box for months. A scientific explanation of my act would be, "*bear or hold in a suspended or inclined manner*". However, my head was only inclined, not suspended. The whole day I walked around with a **hang-dog** expression.

During times of adversity, our friends encourage us to **hang in there**, and demonstrate patience. King Henry V could not possibly have exhorted his army with *Once more unto the breach, etc.* He spent his youth wenching and boozing and suddenly one day found that he was king. As such it is highly doubtful if he had sufficient command over his mother tongue to make rousing speeches. He probably told his soldiers, *"Hang in there guys, we just might win this thing at Agincourt"*.

Many months ago, when an idiot hit my parked Cadillac from behind, necessitating my trashing it (with some help from my insurance company), I **hung on my wife's arm**. I needed all the support I could get.

Many men would appreciate a compliment (from appropriate quarters) that they are **well hung.** But, frankly, that kind of recognition of physical endowment is something not to be concerned about, if one is to believe Dr. Reuben, Dr. Masters and others. Personally I don't have any **hang ups** on this matter. After retirement from active theatre work, I do not find **time hanging heavy** on my hands. Time is not oppressive or burdensome. All the same, I am accused of just **hanging around** in the house and not doing anything. But I suppose I could **hang out** with some of my unemployed friends at the Irish pub close by.

But I am afraid that I just might **hang one on**. The local constabulary would not be very cordial if I chose to drive home after that! Also, I am mortally afraid of a **hangover**. It would not have mattered if I had Jeeves in my employ. He has a concoction, the ingredients of which are a secret. But Bertie Wooster thinks it has dynamite in it, in addition to Worcestershire sauce, and hot pepper in tomato juice. Anyway, a few who have a reputation for '*holding their liquor*' do not get hangovers, I understand. These are tough men and I am told that if I stick to the practice, and work at it, I will **get the hang of it**.

After my retirement, I have, obviously, been very nervous because the health of the exchequer has taken a hit and I am constrained to **hang on to** whatever savings I have. A friend advised me that the thing to do was to consult a financial planner. So I did. He talked about this fund and that, and though I did not understand half of what he said, I **hung on every word**. The recommendation to move to a cheaper place to live is **still hanging**.

Meanwhile, I think of the many things I still want to do. I want to do jury duty and collectively experience what a **hung jury** is like. I want to do some **hang gliding** and soar like a bird. I want to **hang five** on a surf board with the weight of my body forward, toes of one foot turned over the front edge of the board!

In times of adversity it is, perhaps, better for the family to **hang together** and wait for better days to come. I am, however, at the end of my tether. I have been impatiently waiting for some kind of resolution by the courts on a land claim that I had filed many years ago. The rest of the family is advising me to **hang loose** and not get worked up. Maybe I will.

FORWARDS & BACKWARDS

Ever since recorded time, man has tried to excel in his activities. He tries to run faster than anyone else in the world, drive faster, and climb the highest mountain. Or if he gets crazy enough, he enters the Hot Dog Eating Championship, the unbroken record being held by one Joey Chestnut, who ate 62 sausages and buns in ten minutes. Immigrant teenagers in the United States try to master English spelling and win the International Spelling Bee.

But how does one become a palindrome champion? A palindrome, as you know, is a word, phrase or sentence which reads the same forwards or backwards. The most commonly used example is, of course, 'Madam, I'm Adam'. But with a prosaic and mundane effort like that you cannot expect to become a champion. Palindromers at the championship level have to come up with examples that are interesting and intriguing. The sentences should be complex. The one who uses more words has a better chance of winning.

The reigning world palindrome champion is Mark Saltveit.

Mark was first introduced to this phenomenon when he was a kid; his brothers used to call him Kram. He, along with his brothers, had to cram (pun, unintended) into the back seat of the car, bored stiff, during family trips. It was during some of the longer trips that the kids turned to palindromes to pass time. Poop was a very easy and popular one!

During a bout of insomnia when in his twenties, Saltveit remembered how he had filled the hours in the family car. He grabbed a dictionary and set to work. Within hours he had written his first palindrome that most people could not achieve in a month or maybe, ever. He called it **"The Brag of the Vain Lawyer"**. It read, **"Resoled in Saratoga, riveting in a wide wale suit, I use law, Ed. I, wan, ignite virago, tar a snide loser."**

A great palindrome, in Saltveit's estimation, is a little weird. It should be basically grammatical and follow basic rules of language use, but more importantly should tell a story or create an absurd image in the reader's head.

"Take the following example, **Enid and Edna dine,**" he says. "It is a perfectly good palindrome. There's nothing flawed about the English. It's just boring. Now tweak it just a bit, and you've got this: **Dennis and Edna sinned.**"

A few interesting palindromes:

A man, a plan, a cat, a ham, a yak, a yam, a hat, a canal Panama!

Are we not pure? "No sir!" Panama's moody Noriega brags. "It is garbage!" Irony dooms a man; a prisoner up to new era.

VERBING

The other day at the supper table I wondered loudly what the origin of the word 'dystopia' might be. I knew that it was the opposite of 'utopia'—a word coined by Thomas More. Mr. More was offering a blue print for an ideal society with no crime or poverty.

The son offered a solution. "Why don't you google the word, dad?" he said. "I thought 'google' was a noun," I replied.

Observant people would have noticed that I had packed a lot of sarcasm in my statement.

The fact is that I don't like people taking liberties with the language and coining word and phrases at will. "One does not '**chair**' or '**table**' or '**spoon**' anything", I continued after banging the table (with my spoon).

I must clarify that I am the quintessential 'autocrat of the breakfast table' as conceived by Oliver Wendell Holmes, the famous American jurist. That is where the inspiration for banging on the table comes from. When we had a rectangular table, presiding over the brood was easy. Now we have a round table and I remind myself of a story told about J.B.Priestly. There was a special dinner in honor of Mr. Priestly, and they had reserved a seat at the centre of the table. But the chief guest was a bit late; the guests were all seated at the head table. Eventually he arrived and chose to sit at the end of the table, closest to the entrance. The organizers came up to him and told him he had a place reserved for him at the centre of the table. "Where I sit is the centre of the table," he said.

But I digress.

The daughter picked up on my "pre-thumping" statement and said, "Of course you **chair** a meeting, **table** motions. And in cricket, a game that you are fond of and which does not make any sense to anyone, the player **bowls** the ball, other guy **bats,** sometimes for the whole day to produce 17 runs, and eventually **spoons** a catch."

The daughter was not done with me yet. She said, "You are such an avid reader of the Bible. Why don't you check out the Book of Isaiah? You will see that in a verse announcing judgment upon the Ethiopians, it says, *"The fowls shall summer upon them and all the beasts of the earth shall winter upon them."*

I recalled Mike Huckabee, Bible thumping Presidential wannabe, on the campaign trail, trying to differentiate himself from his Ivy League rivals, "For my family, summer was never a verb. We never summered anywhere."

I don't care who says it, but the word 'summering' is obscene.

My kids are millennials, and I am typical 20th century, averse to people taking liberties to vilify a beautiful language. To me the word **cool** does not mean **acceptance** or **attestation.** It is the opposite of **hot.** For any other connotation there might be, I prefer to employ words like **great, good show,** or **keep it up.**

Going back to 'dystopia' I prefer if people said, "Look it up on google" rather than asking me '**to**' google.

Way back in my childhood, I was taught the difference between a noun (person, place or thing) and a verb (action word). With such a tidy definition, it was easy to spot the difference. Not so in adulthood where we were asked to **foot** the bills or **dialogue** with political opponents or '**estimate**' the cost of whatever (and come up with a good **estimate**!). Chances are that we did not cringe at the sight of those verbed nouns because we were used to them.

To be fair, though, "The 'verbing' of nouns is as old as the English language," says Patricia O' Connor the author of **Woe Is I: The Grammarphobe's Guide to Better English in Plain English.** "In fact," she says, "according to experts 20% of all English verbs were originally nouns. Since 1900 about 40% of all of our new verbs have come from nouns. This is called **denominalization,** which is the technical term for converting a noun into a verb."

As I said we have accepted many of the words that have gone through the process. **Attack, benefit, dial, guard, hope, milk, whip,** and **yield** are only a few of the examples of over 460 words in common parlance.

I am sorry if I take a while before accepting 'google' as a verb. Chalk it up to having born in the wrong century.

GOING DUTCH

While browsing through the library downstairs, I chanced upon a book on exotic flowers and one of the examples was a flower called the Dutchman's pipe (see picture below).

Obviously the name has nothing to do with the Dutch or a pipe!

It is fascinating to think of how much the word 'Dutch' has crept into English, creating many idiomatic expressions. I dare say that there is no other country or community that can claim this dubious honor!

A few months after we had immigrated to Canada, I ran into someone I had recently met and he said, "Let us do lunch tomorrow." I must admit that I had not heard the expression before. I was used to "Let's go for lunch tomorrow." Or something similar. But more surprise was in store. We met in a restaurant and at the end he took the bill and added the tip and said, "We will **go Dutch**; and so, let me see, my share is $..."

I was quite surprised. Good thing I had enough cash on me! In other words, I had a '**Dutch treat**' because I paid for the food myself. As I said, there are many expressions involving the nation, some of them not exactly flattering. For instance, '**Dutch courage**' is something you don't want to have. It is a kind of 'artificial' courage that you display after having consumed more alcohol than you can handle for example. It would be Dutch courage if you attacked a policeman in your inebriated state! You would be '**in Dutch**' with the law.

When I was growing up, an elderly uncle used to visit us. He used to arrive at noon and so naturally we fed him. After lunch he would stretch himself on the sofa, stay on for afternoon tea and leave. But during his stay, he would give gratuitous advice and suggestions on everything that came up for discussion – be it an impending marriage, planting crops, redecorating the house or garbage disposal. Free advice. Such people are called '**Dutch uncles**'.

In most auctions, the auctioneer starts off with a reasonable price for the item and hopes that bidders increase the price. But in a **Dutch auction**, the bidding starts at a very high price which is progressively reduced until a buyer is found!

A medico that I go to occasionally talks so very fast that I find it difficult to understand this person. He speaks **Double Dutch.**

One could give respectability to women in the sex trade by calling them **Dutch wives** or **Dutch widows.** But consoling someone who has had a serious misfortune by saying, "Things could have been much worse." is **Dutch comfort.**

'All that glitters is not gold" is especially true of an alloy of copper and zinc. It has the sheen of gold, is malleable and ductile just like gold. It is called **Dutch metal.**

A frog is sometimes referred to as **Dutch nightingale!**

There are many more expressions. **Dutch act** (suicide), **Dutch concert** (noise and uproar), **Dutch generosity** (being stingy)…

An enterprising man called Sjoerd Mullender has collected over 50 expressions involving the word 'Dutch'. I am not sure if other countries have inspired similar expressions. Research revealed nothing except **Indian summer and India(n) ink.** For the benefit of some of the readers overseas, Indian summer describes unseasonably warm, dry weather in the autumn.

I apologize to my dear Dutch friends if this article bristles. Take heart, your contribution to this world is wonderful, especially tulips, rijsttafel, van Gogh and Vermeer.

ENGLISH MANGLED

There are many hospitals in Toronto, obviously, and many people would say that Mount Sinai Hospital provides 'Cadillac care'. I go to this body shop myself, but qualifying the care with the name of the GM product irritates me. I would have preferred "Bentley care' or 'Ferrari care' or something exotic like that.

Anyway, this great institution practises the caste system. Yes, pilgrims, I did say caste system. Obviously, you have your eyebrows raised.

I am not suggesting that there are Brahmins, Sudras and such, though some of the operatives might feel that they belong to those groups. Let me explain.

The edifice has, I believe 24 floors, and who do you think occupies the penthouse floor? The CEO and his staff. There are also the offices of Board members, Board Room, a lecture hall, a lounge and overnight accommodation for visiting dignitaries. Or so I am told. If you, as a CEO, get paid a million dollars a year with a generous car allowance and six months paid vacation, you deserve the penthouse suite as well, I suppose.

The floors below are designated according to hierarchical status. The loony doctors are somewhere on the 22nd floor, the Neurologist, I believe, a floor below, the Cardiologist on the 18th. Ambulatory care, optical care and the care for the choppers are all on the 4th. So are the Pathologist and his labs.

I am sure you have seen how the caste system is operating here, and it would be crystal clear when you go to the basement. Two levels below the main floor you see 'Audiology'! The lowest of the low! To add insult to injury this floor also has a restaurant and large dining space.

I have a pair of ears like all of you, but my family says that they are just ornamental and don't serve any useful purpose. True. But to make my own life less miserable I stick two hearing aids ($2500 bucks a piece!) the size of a large kidney bean into my ears every day. They are a miniature p.a. system of microphones, loudspeakers, volume control and so on. And periodically I have to go to the bowels of the venerable institution to get them tweaked.

It was by accident that, while walking to the office of the audiologist, that I noticed a somewhat strange legend on a door. It said "Female Lockers" (see picture below).

female lockers

At first blush it looks innocuous enough. But if you are a grammarian, it stops you and makes you ponder. Which I did, because I am one of those unfortunate people. Unlike Latin or French, English does not *generally* assign genders to nouns. (Two exceptions come to mind: countries and ships.) **Locker,** a feminine noun?! Like mare or doe or vixen it belongs to the female sex? Surely it has to be a blooper.

I could not help but think think of the many, many instances of mangled English that I have come across during my travels or those that I have read in various documents over the years.

En route Manila on a United Nations assignment, I was routed through Tokyo for orientation purposes and I was staying at one of the better hotels downtown. When I went to the bathroom, I saw the following notice: **It is forbidden to steal hotel towels, please; but if you are not a person do such a thing, please not to read notice.** And when I mentioned this to an American with whom I happened to share the breakfast table the next day, he took out the documents he had signed before renting a car. Among the tips on how to drive in Tokyo, was the following: **When passenger on foot heave into sight, tootle horn. Trumpet him melodiously at first, but if he still obstacles your passage, then tootle him with vigor.**

While on the same assignment, I had to go to a town called Sigma, and I paid a courtesy call to the mayor. When I was leaving the office, I could not help noticing the instruction on the wall: **Turn off the lights when not in use.**

The Secretariat of the European Commission (EC) had, many years ago, a senior official who was an Englishman. He ordered those of his staff who travelled in Europe, and to those overseas countries where English is a foreign language, to collect all examples of tortured English. These are displayed on bulletin boards in the lobby of EC's center, the Borschette office complex in Belgium. Here are a few examples.

An Acapulco hotel reassures guests about drinking water: **The manager has personally passed all the water that is served here.

A campsite in Germany warned: **It is strictly forbidden on our campsite that people of different sex, for instance men and women, live together in one tent unless they are married to each other for that purpose.

A Zurich hotel with similar worries offered this solution: **Because of the impropriety of entertaining guests of the opposite sex in the bedroom, it is suggested that the lobby be used for this purpose.

A notice in a Norwegian cocktail lounge states: **Ladies are requested not to have babies and children in the bar.

A tailor on the Greek island of Rhodes couldn't guarantee that he could finish the summer suits ordered by tourists on time. How did he decide to handle the situation? **Because in big rush we will execute customers in strict rotation.

A sign in a zoo in Budapest says: **Please don't feed the animals. If you have any suitable food, give it to the guard on duty.

In Nigeria a booklet issued by the Public Health Department suggests: **If your baby does not thrive on cold milk, boil it.

One could say that in the examples given, the assault on English was perpetrated by those whose mother tongue is some other language. The native speakers of English are also prone to make mistakes, but one does not expect a person who has been to Yale to make Mrs. Malaprop look like an amateur.

George W Bush, the 43rd President of the United States had such great difficulty in English usage that while he was in office, the verbal slip-ups were very common. A man called Jacob Weisberg started gathering the mangled use of English by the President, and gathered more than 500 Bush-isms over nine years. Here are a few juicy ones.

**Our enemies are innovative and resourceful and so are we. They never stop thinking about new ways to harm our country and our people and neither do we.

**I know how hard it is for you to put food on your family.

**We will let our friends be the peacekeepers and the great country called America will be pacemakers.

**Families is where our nation finds hope, where wings take dream.

**One of the great things about books is sometimes there are fantastic pictures.

**I am looking forward to a good night's sleep on the soil of a friend (on the prospect of visiting Denmark).

Un

No, pilgrims, I am **not** talking about the august body in which I was junior diplomat for over ten years until 2004.

Before I go any further, let me tell you that I am very upset.

Indeed, I am angry.

The reason for this is the way cyber culture is savaging the language of Shakespeare, Milton and Faulkner.

I am sure you are one of the many unfortunate people who get mail ending with the acronym 'lol'. I have to admit that I had for a long time no clue what it meant. Being naïve I thought it stood for '**labor of love**' or '**laundry of luddites**' or something like that. Then an expert in cyber language told me that it stands for '**laughing out loud**'.

Really????

This was some time ago.

If you are like many other victims, I guess that your inbox is inundated every day with rubbish. The saving grace is that on the last page of many of these documents, in miniscule font, you will get the notification that if you don't like to get the stuff, you could '**unsubscribe**'. It was a novel way of using the negative prefix, I thought. Then my daughter told me that

I could '**unfriend**' several of the Facebook friends who insist on telling me how they enjoyed afternoon tea or post pictures of the new chair they bought on sale. One person very kindly informed me that during the weekend he was going to clean up the clutter in the garage. Another told me that she was particularly ecstatic that day because her cat smiled at her. About 12 people 'liked' it.

But the following headline in Politico, the Newsmagazine (June 6, 2016) really got my goat.

Under fire, FBI undeletes ISIL mentions in Orlando 911 transcript

Undelete? Seriously??

Would it not be more 'adult' if they said 'reinserted'?

English, of course, has many prefixes for negative denotations. **De-,** (deregulate), **dis-** (disagree), **in-** (inaccurate), **il-** (illegible), **im-** (impatient), **ir-**(irresponsible), **mis-** (mislead) etc. But trust the English language to come up with kooky conventions!! For instance, one of the first lessons in chemistry had declared that the gas hydrogen was highly inflammable, meaning easily set on fire. But I was very confused when during my first week in Canada, I saw a truck carrying gasoline screaming by and on the side of the body it said "**Flammable**". Further research revealed that the National Fire Protection Association in the 1920's urged Americans to start using the word 'flammable' to avoid confusion and prevent fires because they thought that people might mistake 'inflammable' as meaning not being able to burn!

Another expression that defies logic has to do with the word 'interested'. While **'uninterested'** means not interested, bored, indifferent, **'disinterested'** means impartial or unprejudiced.

But 'undeleted', *imnsho*, is taking things too far.

Cyber culture is going to be responsible for the death of another time honored convention in punctuation: the 'period' or 'full stop'.

I recall reading **"Ulysses"** by James Joyce as part of the requirements for an English course. I was astonished to see that the last 45 pages consisted of **one sentence.** No punctuation marks whatever. Later it was explained to us that Joyce was employing what is called "stream of consciousness", a literary style in which the character's thoughts, feelings and reactions are depicted in a continuous flow. We don't think in sentences. Thought is regarded as a succession of ideas and images constantly moving forward in time.

Joyce was a genius. Not so much all these millennials, whose latest aberration of dropping the 'full stop' is a product of their punctuation-free, staccato sentences, a trend fueled by the freewheeling style of Facebook, WhatsApp and Twitter.

I am angry.

P.S. I had already given finishing touches to the article when I saw an obscene use of internet English in Politico (May 31, 2017). The magazine was highlighting brides who embrace what is called 'counter culture' and wore wedding dresses whose designs were a clear departure from tradition.

The headline said, "31 brides that you can't **unsee**".

I rest my case.

Men (and women too)
And Manners

MEN (WOMEN TOO) AND MANNERS

Greek Sophist Protagoras (490-420 BCE) is credited with the statement **Man is the measure of all things**. A simple annotation of this would be that each person has his/her own individual truth. The principle is called **Relativism**. Truth is relative and differs according to each individual.

It is this sense of 'relativism' that prompts man to do (or not do) things. Thus he might choose to paint the living room bright red, eat spinach or broccoli with breakfast, commit petty and not so petty crimes, ignore the delicate balance of nature, produce children out of wedlock or chop the head off of someone who does not share his religious beliefs.

This section is a deeper look at what people do – be it right or wrong.

Mark Twain said, "The fact that man knows right from wrong proves his intellectual superiority to other creatures; but the fact that he can do wrong proves his moral inferiority to any creature that cannot".

Beheading those who do not subscribe to your religious or political beliefs is relativism taken to absurd limits.

THE GARAGE SALE

When spring rolls in, in addition to hay fever and other discomforts, a deadly malady afflicts ordinary Canadians.

It is called the Garage Sale.

This affliction wreaks havoc on human relations. Perfectly happy married couples have been known to seek legal help as a prelude to separation and perhaps, eventual divorce.

The Garage Sale is a phenomenon where people, during any given shopping trip, pick up an article which they think they desperately need, for, say, twenty dollars, and sell it after five or six years (together with the dust) for five. Usually. This item after being used once or twice is relegated to the basement storage—which is where it collects dust.

Never did I realize that this urge would hit ME. But it did. It happened when Matilda, my wife, was trying to find something—a coffee grinder, I believe—purchased several years ago, because someone told her that the only way to enjoy coffee is to use freshly ground coffee beans. So we bought it and after a month or so promptly stopped using it because we had quickly understood it was much easier to use coffee powder.

Anyway, to get at the coffee grinder, several other dust covered items had to come off the shelf. Pots, pans, cutlery, flower vases, baskets, a fondue set, fruit juicers, a rice cooker....a bewildering variety of things for which we paid MONEY. The sight of all these items spread on the floor gave her the idea. Why don't we have a garage sale?

A shudder passed through my system, and so I said, we don't have a garage – hoping that would discourage her from going ahead with the idea.

"Don't be silly. We will call it a yard sale," she said.

The first step was to survey the total collection and decide which ones should go. I wrote the list, while she 'decided'!!

At one stage I bleated, "Who is going to lift all these things, take them out and arrange them?"

"Well, Ronnie is here. He will help."

The said Ronnie is her son, by her first or second marriage, I forget. This individual has always intrigued me. He is 25 years old, weighs over 200 pounds, and spends most of his time in the basement watching TV or playing video games. Oh yes, he drinks my beer too. I have not seen him do any work of any kind. His mother dotes on him. One day she said, "Isn't he an angel?"

I said, "God has not created wings strong enough to lift this angel off the ground."

Of course, I said this *sotto voce*.

The next step was pricing the articles. Now here's the rub. While most people say that they want to 'get rid of things' they also want to make a lot of money. We had agreed that we would price alternate pieces.

So she said, six dollars for the turntable. I was supposed to accept it, but moral indignation made me say, "You can't ask six dollars for an item that does not work properly!" She reminded me of the 'contract' and so I just shut up. When my turn came, I priced a TV table which had only three castors, at two dollars. Unfortunately, at that exact time, Ronnie walked by, *en route* raiding the fridge for MY beer, and gave his opinion. "Pops, you are crazy to sell this for two bucks. You should get at least six." (I hate it when he addresses me as 'Pops'.) Matilda promptly agreed.

The pricing completed, the next step was to announce the dates of the sale. The trend these days seems to be Friday and Saturday. So I composed an ad and went to the local (and only) newspaper office on the Wednesday prior to the sale. Two young ladies greeted me with a smile, and one of them proceeded to count the words in the ad, and declared that it will cost me $44. I argued that their advertised rates were $22 for one insert. But I had ten extra words and so it would be double. So I had to do some fancy editing and brought the ad within the limits set by the paper. I also said it was a Moving Sale. (After reading the ad our neighbour, the Potters, asked me if we were, indeed, moving. I said that we were moving, yes, but moving things from the basement to the yard.)

On Thursday, the process of lugging things from all the rooms began. Ronnie suddenly developed a back ache, and so his mother relieved him of his duties. Naturally the job fell on my shoulders, though I am the one with the bad back!

Finally, the day dawned, and it turned out to be a very blustery day. I had the cash box ready with loonies, quarters, dimes, nickels. I had borrowed a cashbox from one of my friends. I had set up my station. I was looking forward to the role of the cashier.

I must say that I was sort of excited, having never had the experience before. The sale was not supposed to start until ten in the morning but people started walking in at eight!

I am convinced that there is a special breed of people who relish going to garage sales. It almost appears as though there is the professional garage sale aficionado. The behaviour pattern of these people is something that psychologists should study.

There are people who bargain even when an article worth $150 is priced at $15. Will you take $2? This for a leather coat which I had never worn because the sleeves were too long! Then there are those who pick up everything in sight. There are people who just walk through the garage or the yard. These people must have extra sensory capabilities, because they are able to decide if they want something by striding through. This takes about 30 seconds.

On Saturday around two p.m. the traffic seemed to lessen and I suggested that perhaps we should wind up the sale. Ronnie who happened to overhear this said that a lot of people came during the last hour, and so we should wait.

I said, "Really?"

Eavesdroppers would have noticed that the question was loaded with sarcasm!

Finally, it was decided that the sale should close. And one look at the stuff around me told me that we had not moved much. The wife could not resist the temptation to count the spoils of the day, and after a while announced that we had made sixty dollars! It was not easy for her to hide her disappointment because she had hoped that there would be enough money made to purchase a new dishwasher!

So the junk went back into the house. Ronnie's backache had persisted and so he just supervised the transfer, much to my irritation.

By Sunday afternoon the last spoon and scarf and spade and box of rusty nails, and the weed'n feed bar and incomplete set of crockery and dried flowers and beaten up suitcases and the Betamax and assorted junk went back to the original places.

Our house is still cluttered as ever.

"Never again," I said.

Again, only *sotto voce.*

WARPS AND WEFTS

I am not quite sure when man decided to wear clothes as we know them.

If we are to go by the Bible, Genesis 3:7 says, "Then the eyes of both (Adam and Eve) opened and they knew that they were naked. And they sewed fig leaves together and made themselves loincloths." And according to Genesis 3: 21 "The Lord God made garments of skin for Adam and his wife, and clothed them."

To assert that Adam was the forebear of the primitive man who wandered about the Serengeti plains in Tanzania would be opening up the debate between creationists and evolutionists, and this I am not prepared to do. But it is unlikely that the primitive man of Serengeti used fig leaves, ever. For one thing there are no fig trees in Tanzania as far as I know. At least not that I have seen.

But it is reasonable to assume that primitive man had a lot of hair on his body for protection, if that is what clothes are for. It could not have been to be protected from the elements, because in Africa, it is generally always warm. Of course, it rained, but when that happened he could easily take shelter in the cave.

It must have been when he decided to migrate that he was exposed to cold – in Europe and parts of Asia. It is logical to assume that when the need to cover himself was acute, he probably used hides of the animals which he had hunted for food. I am not sure if he believed in family planning or if there was, indeed, a Mao-like leader who issued an edict that the family can have only one child. Whatever the case was, I suspect the hide of a mid-sized pachyderm would have been ample to create coverings for the whole family.

Obviously the clothes that people wear have changed over the centuries. Ancient Egyptians produced linen around 5,500 BC, while the Chinese likely started producing silk around 4,000 BC. The history of clothing and the changes over the centuries are beyond the scope of this article. But 1872, perhaps, must be considered one of the most important years in the history of clothing because that year a German immigrant to the United States called Levi Straus manufactured a material called denim with which he made jeans. One shudders to think what we would have done all these years without jeans. The versatility and the advantages of owning a pair of jeans are also beyond the scope of this blog.

But what is noteworthy is the evolution of the original pair of jeans into the most modern version which is like a second skin. It almost looks as though it has been poured on to the body (see picture below).

The picture below demonstrates how one could get into the garment.

But what is astonishing to a rank traditionalist like me is the sight of perfectly decent looking jeans ripped here and there, deliberately I might add, to expose skin (see picture below).

A meticulously ripped pair of jeans.

In a weak moment I thought that I needed to be a 'cool dude' like any other guy and rip a pair of jeans.

The first thing to do was to buy a pair because I have never worn a pair of jeans in my life. It made me uneasy to rip a perfectly good garment, but having decided to do it, I was not going to back off. Of course, I had no clue of how to go about it. I knew that the **warps** (longitudinal strands) are blue and the **wefts** (lateral strands) are white. Fashion demands that you expose the wefts, which meant that in a rip the blue ones are to go. Mercifully, I chanced upon on an excellent video on how to do it properly. In this video a very self-assured young woman demonstrated how to make the perfect rip. Depending on how many rips you want and how complicated the design of the rip is, the process could be very time consuming.

On a different note. I believe people wear different clothes for different purposes. Ever since we became *civilized*, it has become an unwritten law that we 'dress for the occasion'. For instance, one does not go for a job interview wearing tank tops and Bermuda shorts. If you get lucky enough to get to meet the President or the Pope, I think it would be discourteous to appear in a pair of tattered jeans. Or if you are the newscaster in a reputable TV station and you are interviewing someone.

I recall the occasion when Steve Fonyo was being inter-viewed on one of the networks. Fonyo, as you might recall, had lost his left leg to cancer when he was 12 years old. At the age of 18, to raise money for cancer research, he embarked on a cross Canada marathon on March 31, 1984 and com-pleted it on May 29, 1985 having covered over 7,900 km. He raised over 15 million dollars for cancer research. But he soon became a troubled person, running afoul of the law, getting addicted to drugs and such. His tragic life is the subject of a documentary called **Hurt** which was one of the most highly rated documentaries at the Toronto International Film Festival a couple of years ago. During the interview I was appalled when I saw the interviewer wearing torn jeans! Maybe it was the "cool" thing to do. The camera picked it up several times as if to attract our attention just in case we missed it.

MIDDLE CLASS BLUES

I belong to the middle class. I know this because my dad told me so when I was 9 or 10. I am sure he did not use the term 'middle class' because English was not the medium of communication in our house. I don't know exactly what the corresponding term in our native lingo is. But I got the sense that I was not poor and also not rich.

The circumstances that led to this revelation are very clear in my mind. I grew up on the outskirts of the city, far away from civilization. We had no paved roads, no electricity, and no running water. Practically village conditions. I was an astute kid and noticed that there were many families around me who did not have homes as large as mine. They wore dirty and sometimes tattered clothes and did what was called 'menial' jobs. The kids did not go to school. I was told that they were poor.

But then, I also noticed that there were other families living in much larger houses than ours. Their property was also larger. They had many more coconut trees, mango trees etc. Some of them had carriages drawn by two bullocks. In fact, one had a carriage drawn by a single horse. This particular man did not go to work. My father went to work every day, and I had a notion that he got 'paid' for his work. This money was used to buy food and clothes and such. So I had wondered how this man who owned the carriage could afford to live, and maintain a large house, without any apparent source of income. This was baffling.

So I asked my father to explain this confusing scenario and at that time he said that the 'horse' guy was 'rich'.

The people who lived in huts were 'poor'. And we were somewhere in between called 'middle class'.

After getting my degree I started working as a teacher and I was paid 50 rupees a month. That is the equivalent of one dollar today. After two years I took leave of absence and got a degree in teaching and this resulted in a pay hike. I got 60 rupees.

One day my father told me that the Federal government was recruiting auditors and that I should apply for the job. My protest that I had no head for figures was not heeded. So I applied for the job and got picked. Overnight my salary shot up to a whopping 120 rupees, including what was called Dearness Allowance, the meaning of which I did not understand. I still don't.

But this sudden rise in emoluments did not make me rich, I don't think. I could now buy a tennis racket, but that was about it. I slogged away as an auditor exposing people who played fast and loose with government funds. I can't say that I enjoyed the work, but the income was good. I supplemented my income by teaching in a private college part time. It's lucky I didn't get

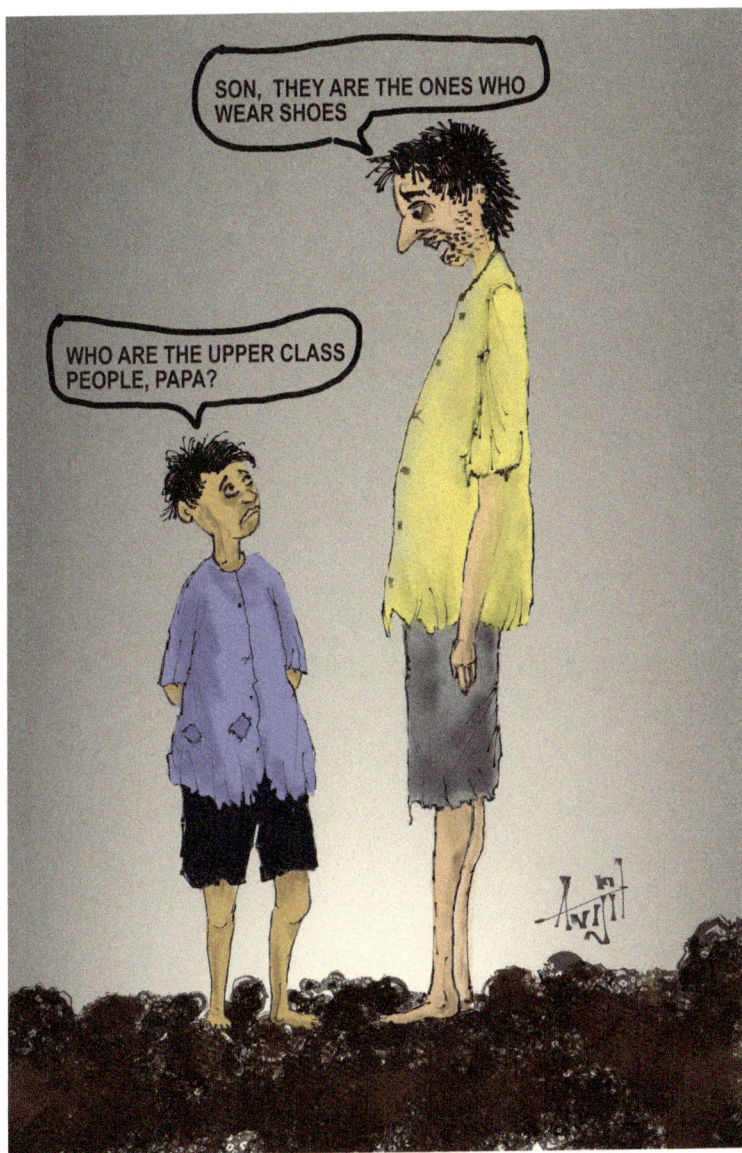

caught and suspended, because Federal employees were not allowed to accept other remunerative jobs while in service.

Even with all this boost to the family exchequer, I was still middle class. I was reaching the conclusion that teachers and auditors did not get rich. I was settling down to spend retirement as a middle class man when I saw an ad in the local newspaper, from the British government, inviting applications from candidates to join the Civil Service and teach in the colonies. The salary offered was astronomically high in terms of Indian rupees, and so I threw my hat in. (I know, I know, Indians don't wear hats).

I got picked and was sent to Uganda and I was sure I would graduate to the next higher social stratum.

But, alas, it was not to be. The civil servants were not rich. The business people were. The British bosses also were. I managed to buy a car but my neighbor had three. So here I was, back on familiar middle class grounds.

When we decided to immigrate to Canada in 1965, I got a job even when I was overseas, and this particular job as a teacher offered me 10,000 dollars a year. And I told myself, 'Finally!'

But, boy, was I in for a surprise! In a few years I noticed that I did not own a boat or motorhome or a cottage by the lake.

I did not play golf or take skiing vacations. But I was introduced to another rung in the social ladder, two in fact – upper middle class and lower middle class. And the middle class still in the middle. To date, I don't know the difference.

After changes in jobs, pay scale revisions, adjustment to cost of living, factoring inflation and such I did not notice any change. When I retired, I was still middle class. I am still middle class, although getting older can be a sure-fire path to poverty. That has been keeping me up at night.

But I have a message for you all middle-classers. The politicians care for us more than they care for the others. Trust me, they do. They have our ultimate good in their hearts and are constantly striving to raise our standards of living. This mission is more eloquently articulated during elections. They aver that the middle class is the backbone of the country.

This makes me feel good because I know that politicians are honest, sincere people and they mean what they say and say what they mean. Thank the Lord for small mercies.

To my point about being unsure about what exactly makes a person belong to the category of middle class, I read that David Cameron, the ex-British Prime Minister also belongs to the middle class. This was declared in one of his speeches which was reported in the Toronto Globe and Mail. "British Prime Minister David Cameron set off a flurry of very British excitement this week when he referred to members of the 'sharp elbowed middle classes like my wife and me' at a government-subsidized daycare center. Noting his background and circumstances—son of a multimillionaire banker, educated at Eton & Oxford, married to the eldest daughter of a hereditary aristocrat—British pundits are perplexed."

Cameron's net worth is $50 million, if you are wondering.

BURNOUT

I should not be surprised if you don't know what the acronym CCOHS stands for. It is the Canadian Centre for Occupational Health and Safety. This institution "promotes the social well-being—physical, psycho-social, and mental health—of working Canadians by providing information, training, education, management systems and solutions."

A very lofty mandate, in my opinion.

I very carefully looked at the services offered by this organization. There is one area of 'hazard' that does not seem to have been addressed and that is the after-effects of very hard work, popularly known as *burnout.*

Tough thing, this burnout. Obviously it is the result of allowing work to get the better of you, denying you time for other pleasurable activities like taking your kid to a ball game, going on a picnic during weekends, fishing or whatever.

I know of a teacher who was 'burnt out' every year around late October/early November, i.e. about 40 working days after the school had opened!!

Several professors at the college where I worked had complained to me that they were over-worked and expressed genuine fear that they were heading towards a nervous breakdown, which is the next stage after burnout. And these scholars taught about 12 hours a week! That is approximately two and a half hours a day. Back-breaking toil, if you ask me!

To all those who think they are in imminent danger of a breakdown, I have to tell you this: Enjoy yourself, you HAVE plenty of time.

When people struck by paranoia say that they are over worked and complement the statement with, *I just don't have the time for doing anything else,* I don't believe them. Only five per cent of the working class don't have free time at all, according to a recent survey held in England. The rest stated that they have plenty of time on their hands for outside activities.

Of course, this is in England. I am sure it is different in Canada. Try as hard as I might, I could not access any Canadian statistics on this matter; but I can't imagine that the data would be substantially different. The reason is clear. The statisticians are overworked, possibly heading towards a mental breakdown.

It appears that this malady does not afflict blue collar workers. So carpenters, auto workers, waiters and such do their 8 hours a day, go to a pub, have a beer to unwind and are ready to go home and spend time on whatever turns them on. No burnout. But teachers, lawyers, doctors, IT project managers and such seem to be more susceptible to this.

I must admit that I have not met a single professional who has readily admitted that he/she had a lot of free time in a day.

Or is it fashionable to say that one is overworked to avoid being perceived as lazy?

Politicians, more than others, feel that their work is more important than anybody else's and that their workload is greater. So they believe they work harder than others. Ask any Senator in Canada. I can understand this. Think of all the travel involved. Think of all the 300 dollar lunches, all those 'working holidays' in the Bahamas. Tough life, really.

Personally, my firm belief is that there is no need to work hard and have a nervous breakdown. President Reagan, (the actor cowboy turned President) who is widely recognized as one of the most idle occupants of the White House in decades, was also, arguably, one of the more 'successful' US presidents. He had also the dubious honour of nodding off in the presence of the Pope. Anyway, regardless of what happened around him, every evening he would not be denied the viewing of a movie in the White House theatre. President George W Bush (the real cowboy turned President) broke all existing records. He spent more time in his ranch or in Kennebunkport where his father lived or Camp David than in the White House. In August 2001, he was on vacation for a whole month! Iraq and the Congress be damned, he said.

I am not sure whether Reagan or Bush really liked the work of being the President. They enjoyed the trappings, but work? I don't think so.

I can relate to this because I myself hate hard work. I must hasten to add that it was Bertrand Russell who inspired me in this matter. More about Russell later. I love being idle and to help me accomplish this during my tenure as an administrator I got sterling advice from one of my colleagues. When I complained to him that I found it difficult to cope up with the volume of work, he said, "Don't be an idiot. Delegate."

"Meaning what?" quoth I.

The answer was revealing. "Let others do your work for you. They will feel important that you have given them responsibility. If they do well, you get all the credit. If they don't, blame them, fire them and get some other wannabe to do your job. Meanwhile play golf or raise bees or renovate the basement or whatever."

This is called **organized diminution of work**. I did not coin this expression. Bertrand Russell did. In his excellent essay **In Praise of Idleness** he wrote, "The road to happiness and prosperity lies in an organized diminution of work." Russell was not only a great fan of idleness (paradoxical in a man so fanatically productive) but he was also firmly of the view that having a belief that your work is terribly important is one of the key symptoms of an approaching nervous breakdown.

Take it easy. Believe it or not, the workplace just might go on without you.

It appears that burnout is not a major issue in Japan. This is because of a custom called *"inemuri"*. It means "sleeping on duty". In most countries sleeping on the job isn't just frowned upon, it may get you fired. But in Japan napping in the office is common and culturally accepted. It is a practice that has been in vogue for at least 1,000 years. So professors can, in the middle of a lecture, decide to lie down and take a nap. In the long run, burnout becomes a non-issue.

There **is** something to be said about Asian cultures.

RAGE

No, I am not referring to Dylan Thomas who exhorted his dying father, "Do not go gentle into that good night, rage, rage against the dying of the light."

No, this is a different kind of rage.

February 8, 1994 would become a memorable day for Oscar winning actor Jack Nicholson. He was driving in North Hollywood and at a red light, he got out of the car, took an iron club out of his golf bag, walked up to the Mercedes Benz just ahead of him and bashed in the windscreen and the roof. The bewildered owner of the Benz, one Robert Blank, apparently had cut Nicholson off and overtook him at some point. Naturally the great actor was charged with misdemeanor charges of assault and vandalism. Nicholson apologized and paid $500,000 in damages (years later he would play a therapist, counselling Adam Sandler in the black comedy, **Anger Management**). Nothing serves an actor more than a rich and varied emotional memory. The director must have known something about Method Acting!

There are, of course, many instances of this kind of behavior chronicled in the news media. In Toronto, early in

August last year, a young driver was accosted and sprayed in the face with an unknown substance by an irate driver. The victim, naturally, lost control and smashed into two cars parked nearby.

This behavior by drivers is called **Road Rage.** This term was coined in 1988, I believe, and refers to a motorist's extreme anger in response to a perceived injustice committed by other drivers. Those not disposed to violent reactions like Nicholson's satisfy themselves by using the middle finger or resorting to verbal abuse—both fairly innocuous.

Psychologists who have done extensive research on possible misdemeanors by drivers (and sometimes pedestrians) that cause road rage have come up with a pretty substantial list. Google can help you here if you are curious. But what the experts have not been able to determine is who the first kook was who started this or, for that matter, where. Moscow, Istanbul, San Francisco and Mexico City have all been mentioned.

It is refreshing to note that something that was started two decades ago is alive and well.

But the latest rage is what is called **Recliner Rage**, a hot new trend among frustrated air travellers. Those who have travelled by plane, I am sure, are familiar with the following scenario. The pilot has given you permission to unbuckle the seat belts, and you are no longer required to sit upright. You settle down to relish reheated frozen food that is on its way or set up your laptop to do some urgent work. The passenger in front of you suddenly feels the dire need to relax, and converts the chair into a recliner, and pushes the chair back. Sometimes the food tray or the computer is dislodged. It certainly becomes difficult to get up and go to the washrooms. This action by insensitive passengers has given rise to the newest aberration in human behavior, **Recliner Rage**.

A few months ago an outburst over a reclined seat led an American Airlines flight to divert to Boston and according to Associated Press it was at least the second incident in the US that particular week. Passenger Edmund Alexandre became upset when a woman reclined her seat in front of him on the Miami-Paris flight on August 27, 2014. A flight crew member attempting to calm him down had no noticeable effect. Two undercover federal air marshals finally subdued the man and handcuffed him.

Earlier in the week a Delta Airlines flight from New York to Florida made an emergency landing after a dispute between two passengers. The passenger who was trying to sleep with her head on the tray became upset when the person in front of her reclined her seat.

Well, trust innovators to come up with a solution!! You can buy what are called 'Knee Defenders' that help you stop the person sitting in front of you from reclining the seat.

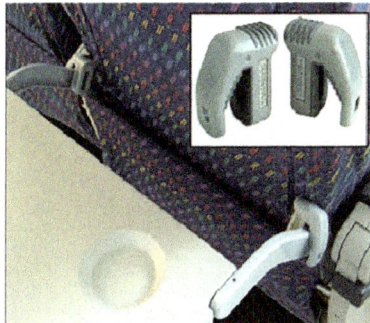

This gadget, available for $21 a pair, will prevent the seat in front of you from reclining and help you keep the legroom space you need to do in-seat exercises while flying. Foot lifts and knee lifts are recommended to promote healthy blood flow to help protect against *deep vein thrombosis*.

But.

Last week two passengers got into a dispute over one of them using the contraption. The flight attendant asked the flyer to remove the device, but he refused, forcing an unscheduled landing.

The FAA does not ban the use of the Knee Defender or such other devices, and it says that it is up to the airlines to ban them, if necessary. All major airlines prohibit their use. Google Consumer Surveys found that 66 per cent of passengers surveyed don't think that the Knee Defender should be permitted. Wait. This means that 34 per cent do.

"D" FOR DECADENCE

Most convenience stores in this country offer you a chance to be rich. To become a millionaire, sometimes 30 times over.

The procedure is very simple. You need to make a modest investment, naturally. No pain, no gain. Mercifully, the investment is not very large, usually under five dollars. You invest the fiver and buy a Lotto ticket. On Saturday you wake up rich. You can do this every week if you wish, but I suspect you would get weary of the exercise.

Thus it was that on a Wednesday last week, I tarried briefly at one of these places. That particular week, I could win 30 million smackeroos. Being a cautious individual, I decided not to fall victim to any sudden impulse and went home to give the whole matter some serious thought.

My first question was that if I won the lottery and survived the initial shock, what exactly would I DO with all that money? I tried to recall how rich people – past and present – spent their wealth. I decided to do some research.

I read that in India Emperor Shah Jahan (he of the Taj Mahal fame) built himself a throne made of gold. The back of the piece of furniture was in the shape of the tail feathers of a peacock. The whole unit was studded with precious stones including the famous Kohinoor. This diamond, by the way, was mined in the southern state of Andhra Pradesh in South India.

The Peacock Throne, as it was called, was taken away to Persia by King Nadir Shah in 1739 I believe. Somehow it travelled a lot back and forth and finally arrived back in India and the Governor General at that time, a man called Lord Dalhousie, thought that the Kohinoor had best be in a safe place. He pried it out of the chair and set it on the crown of the British monarch, where it resides today.

I am too old to organize a heist to get it back and so I kept reading. I learned about the Maharajas of India, for instance, who had a great deal of wealth and knew how to spend it. They were fond of ostentatious living.

One thing they did in addition to covering themselves with precious stones was to own a stable of cars—mostly Rolls Royces. In the first 50 years of the 20th century more than 800 Rolls Royces were exported to India. Anyway, I ruled out the automobile because I don't have a driving license anymore.

King Farouk of Egypt was another person I looked up. He had a very ostentatious style as well. For instance, he consumed 600 oysters a week - that is about 80 a day! This showed because he apparently weighed over 300 pounds. He collected walking sticks and ended up with 1800 of them. He also bought 300 neckties. I don't need a walking stick yet, and I prefer cravats to ties. So Farouk was no help either.

Then I recalled Bill Fletcher once telling me that money is in real estate. Building or buying a house. Not just any house; but something worthy of a freshly minted millionaire. So again I went looking for inspiration. It was not hard to find. I noticed that steel magnate Mukesh Ambani built a 27 storey building for himself in Mumbai, but since the ceilings are very high it is equivalent to 60 floors (see picture below).

He has 168 cars and has committed six floors to parking. He has three helipads just in case three helicopters suddenly descended on him for whatever reason. But my problem was the house looked as though it was based on a model made up of Lego blocks by a school boy. Sure, I wanted something unique, but this wasn't it.

I was at the point of giving up hope when I read that Lionel Messi, the soccer phenom, had hired an architect to build his house in the shape of a soccer ball! His new house will be in Caledonia and the soccer-themed house would be built on a soccer field. The two storey home will look like a giant soccer ball on a rectangular plot and will split the plot into two halves. One half of the plot will have a swimming pool and the other side will have a luxurious lawn (see picture below).

The house will have a grass roof which will be divided up, giving it a quadrant effect from above. And, oh, eventually the number on his jersey, 10, will be visible from the air. I liked it and seriously considered hiring Messi's architect.

When I came down to earth, I realized that I would not be able to afford anything close to what these people have. Ambani spent 1 billion to build his place. I've read that Messi is worth $773 million, so even if he spends 1% of that on his house, I am out of that league!

I decided that the prudent thing to do is to not to buy the lottery ticket, save the $5 and learn to enjoy living in my modest abode. Ambani is welcome to visit, as long as he knows that I don't have anywhere for him to land his helicopter.

IT'S ALL NOMINAL

Design Exchange in Toronto is a non-profit design museum and centre for the advancement of Canadian design. It is located in the historic Toronto Stock Exchange building.

Recently the institution had a distinguished speaker. A lady. As described by Shinan Govani in the Financial Post, she was a "former Polo model turned heiress turned hotelier, designer, author, TV personality, fragrance guru (guruess?) and Princess Diana's bridesmaid."

Her name? **India Hicks.**

Her mother Lady Pamela was the daughter of Lord Louis Mountbatten, the last Viceroy of India, and her father was an English interior decorator and designer, who was noted for the dynamic use of color, and for mixing antiques and contemporary art for his clientele, who included the King of Saudi Arabia, Vidal Sassoon and the Queen herself.

But why he and Lady Pamela would give their daughter the name **India** is beyond me. I know that Lady Pamela's mother Lady Edwina was in love with the country and also its Prime Minister, Mr. Jawaharlal Nehru.

I have been wondering what my life would have been if my father decided to name me after a country. I suppose I could have lived with **Mali or Bali**. But because he was an admirer of Kemal Ataturk, if my father, in a sudden fit of hero worship, had chosen to name me **Turkey**, I would have had a major problem.

I know some parents want to give unique names to their children. But **Zxyrill** or **Typewriter**? I am not making this up. You will find the first name in Alberta and the second in Zimbabwe. I suppose I have to thank the Lord that I was not born in Zimbabwe! Dr Valentin Hristov of the University of Zimbabwe, who is interested in names and has done a lot of research found names such as **Addmore**, **Climate**, **Obey**, **Wander**, **Wireless** and **Ximas** among others.

But even these names pale in comparison with some of the names given by early American puritans according to Bill Bryson, who in his excellent book, **Made in America**, cites examples like **Misericordia**, **Job-Raked-Out-Of-The-Ashes**, **Small-Hope** and **Kill-Sin**.

Closer to home, I have nieces who are known by the names **Baby** and **Mini**. There are Bollywood stars called **Dimple** and **Twinkle**. And speaking of movie stars, Gwyneth Paltrow named her daughter **Apple**.

To all you expectant parents, just in case you have been inspired by this article, here are a few suggestions. For boys: **Jeirjany, Staunche, Rave, Tag** and **Formula**. For girls: **Cannaceae, Millenary, Symphony, and Tear Drop**. Once again, be assured that I did not create these names. There are birth certificates somewhere in the world which would testify to their authenticity.

These names also create problems for the people who are expected to pronounce them. If a parent in Eastern Europe whose last name is **Gwaizdowski** or **Modrzejewski** chose to give the name **Zxyrill** to his son, teachers in Canada, for instance, would find it somewhat difficult to pronounce. And I am speaking of a country where there are people who cannot even pronounce a simple name like "Nayar". I have been called, **Neigher, Naiyyar,** and **Neighyaar.**

And spelling my first name? In another incarnation I was the Chairman of Fine Arts at Grande Prairie Regional College, and I used to get a lot of mail, and occasionally the mail would bring me a letter with a mangled spelling of my name. One day I decided to collect all the variations to my name and I have on file 28. **Sulsarmar Nayar, Sukomar Nayan, Sukimar Nayah, Sukar Nayar, S. Narjar and Sirkumar Nayar** to name a few.

But the most interesting one is **Professor Fukumar Nayar.** I'm sure some of you will have a comment on that one.

To conclude. I am sure you know that Kim Kardashian is married to Kanye West. They named their first child **North.** So the kid will live through life with name **North West!!**

BELCHERS BEWARE

The human body is a complex engine and like all engines it runs on fuel. And like all engines the body spews out waste in many forms. It also makes noises of many kinds. We cough when something gets stuck in our throat (think of an exhaust in a car backfiring). We sneeze when the nostrils are irritated, and with the sneeze the body also discharges fluids. We burp or belch when there is a buildup of gases in the stomach. We fart when the build-up happens farther south. I am not sure if all animals perform the activities mentioned above.

For instance, I am not sure if a dog sneezes. It might cough up anything stuck in its throat. I know cattle fart because the ex-speaker of the United States House of Representatives, John Boehner, told us so. He attributed global warming to millions of cows farting and sending hot gases into the atmosphere. He did not mention anything about bulls or other animals that also might perform this function. I suspect that a herd of elephants would be more culpable than a warren of rabbits. Nothing to do with humans, he asserted.

He was probably right. Think of the billions of animals in the world and it is reasonable to assume that they do, indeed, during the course of the day fart many times, thus causing global warming.

But belching has a complicated history. In Asian and Arabic cultures, it is a social requirement that you belch after a meal, especially if you are a guest. You don't need to say, "Great meal!", as a resounding belch is enough. One recalls the scene in the movie Ben Hur, where Charleston Heston (Ben Hur) is at lunch with Sheikh Ilderim (Hugh Griffith) in his fancy tent. After the meal, the sheikh asks him if he didn't enjoy the meal because he did not hear the obligatory belch from his guest. "On the contrary", replies Hur. The sheikh still has an unhappy face and Hur quickly realizes that he has not done the appropriate thing, and burps loudly, bringing a smile to the granite face of the sheikh.

Where I grew up, in our family it was mandatory to burp after a meal. We were trained to do it. I could do it in 'fifty different sharps and flats' like the rats in Robert Browning's Pied Piper of Hamelin.

But not every country or city accepts belching as a socially acceptable activity. Vienna for one.

Anyone who has visited Vienna would remember that one of the most famous landmarks is the Wiener Prater, a very large amusement park open 24 hours a day, 7 days a week. There are Ferris wheels, roller coaster rides, a bowling alley and a miniature railway to entertain young and old alike. The amusement park is also where you go if you are looking for illicit drugs. This, of course, brings a large contingent of the gendarmes, who patrol the vast park. Obviously, there are many eateries and watering holes as well. Schweizerhaus is one of the more popular restaurants, perhaps, the most well known in Vienna. It is famous for its pork knuckles, beer and potato pancakes. Edin Mehic was one of the bartenders who helped quench the thirst of the public.

It is here where we come to the point. Mehic was fined by police in Vienna for burping after he had lunch. One day, after a gruelling lunch rush, he went out for a bite to eat and as such went to his favorite kebab stand in the park. There he asked for a hot kebab with a lot of onions and a can of coke to wash it down. He went to a nearby bench and sometime during the lunch, he burped somewhat loudly. The coke and the onions did it!

Those who burp (belch) would know that whatever the result, it is a very satisfying action. Mehic was enjoying the afternoon. Then it was that he felt a heavy hand on his shoulder. Turned out to be the local gendarme. The stern mien of the law told Mehic that something was wrong. He was told that he had violated a section of the city by-law which stated that a "decency violation" is subject to fines, and burping in public is one such (see article 29.a.172.6).

Not being schooled in civic statutes, Mehic was very surprised and tried to argue with the policeman, suggesting that he had better try and round up real criminals who were obviously consuming and/or dealing in drugs rather than bugging him.

To no avail. Mehic was guilty of a grave and flagrant violation of the law and he must pay the price for it. He was fined the maximum, on the spot. $77.00—almost his daily wages.

The offended bartender posted a photograph of the official "fine document" on his Facebook page. The post went viral and an outraged public rallied round Mehic and there was an international call for protesting this outrageous act of violation of human rights. Apparently thousands of people assembled on the weekend armed with kebab, onions and beer.

Whether, at a given signal the throng let out a collective belch or not I am not sure.

CRIME AND PUNISHMENT

(With apologies to Dostoevsky)

Like many mortals, I have my weaknesses. One of them is that I am an inveterate day dreamer. The mind goes wool-gathering whenever I am not busy concentrating on things. What if? Could I?

My wish list is long. Very long.

One of the most compelling desires is to commit a crime. Yeah.

Nothing too serious. Something innocuous. Indulging in something that *just* goes beyond the bounds of lawful behaviour. Just.

I am fully aware that if I am convicted I will go to jail. But I won't commit the crime in Canada. I will go to California. Because the Californians have a civilized system called **self-pay** in their prison system. It is more or less like upgrading your flight from tourist to business. You know how you pay a little more and you get to sleep on a seat that stretches into a sort of couch.

So you get convicted of a crime and the judge throws you in the clink. Then, you can negotiate for souped-up accommodation. In essence, instead of being in a small room with iron bars, and with cockroaches as co-habitants, you get a clean room with an attached bathroom, clean sheets, blankets, pillows and such – not quite the Hyatt, but comfortable.

Of course, you have to pay for this extravagance. At press, the going rate is anywhere between $120 and $250 a day. People who have had the opportunity of experiencing this novel form of incarceration say that the accommodation was clean and safe. Most importantly, they did not get harassed by other inmates (called clients). You are allowed to bring in your cell phone. You can bring your laptop and start work on 'the book' that you have always wanted to write. Or learn Spanish.

Depending on your crime you might even be granted a furlough. So you go to work, wherever that might be, and return in the evening.

Relatives and friends are allowed to bring you hot food every day, if that is your wish. Otherwise you share the refectory menu. I guess I will have to settle for that because I have a suspicion that my wife is not going to be thrilled at the prospect of bringing me curry and rice every day.

In Pasadena, I am told, the rooms are full, and there is a waiting list.

Jennifer Steinhauser, who first reported this said, "Many of the self-pay jails operate like velvet-roped night clubs of the corrections world. You have to be in the know to even apply for entry, and even if the court approves your sentence there, jail administrators can operate like bouncers, rejecting anyone they wish."

The typical client is sentenced to a month or two in jail. That is for the kind of crime that I want to commit. There are single night guests, as well as those who stay put for well over a year. One guy wanted to be away from his nagging family and stay for four years at the Santa Ana Correctional Facility.

"Many prisoners, who are charged with nonviolent crimes and typically have no record, are not in the best position to handle themselves to rub shoulders with heavily tattooed giants with bulging biceps," says Professor Goldman of the Loyola Law School. He is talking about criminals like me.

Coming back to my own incarceration, I am confident that Hizzoner would look at my very impressive resume and the reference letter from my ex-boss United Nations Secretary General Kofi Annan and acquit me. He would cite temporary insanity, a mere mental aberration.

If not, I would emulate our own defrocked Lord Black and teach the inmates something. Black taught the inmates history. I can teach drama. In fact, I could even start a theatre group and put on shows like **Hope Is the Thing with Feathers**, which requires an all-male cast. I don't think the place is co-ed, unfortunately. At least I would be guaranteed a captive audience!!

ADDICTION

I have an addiction.

It is after a great deal of introspection that I have decided to admit this. Behavioral scientists maintain that when you have an addiction, it is best to admit it and announce it, instead of keeping it bottled up. Hence my admission.

No, it is not that I have become an alcoholic. I don't do drugs, I have not taken up smoking or chewing tobacco, I have not developed a sweet tooth. No. It is simply that as soon as I wake up in the morning, instead of sipping a cup of tea or coffee, I make a beeline for the computer.

I turn it on and open my inbox. I want to see how many letters I have received. It is usually around 20 at that time of the day. I don't open them until after breakfast, though while breaking the fast I am on tenterhooks as it were, because I want to get to the computer as soon as possible. I silently (and with frustration)

wonder why the wife is taking so long to consume a piece of toast. Of course, she is reading the newspaper as well.

Once the fast is broken, I rinse the plates and such, throw them in the dishwasher ('The cups go on top, Sukumar, pots at the bottom', a disembodied, incorporeal voice admonishes me. 'How many times have I told you?') and reach the comfort of my ergonomic chair.

I see that today I have 23 letters. Many of them are breaking news announcements from the newspapers I read every day. But then I have assorted outfits clamoring for my attention.

Facebook for example. I often get intimations that "X" or "Y" has updated his/her status. In this case the word 'status' is a misnomer. For instance, I got a notification the other day that this particular correspondent found a rat in his house. I kid you not. How the appearance of a rodent in his dwelling actually changed his status, I don't know. I don't know his status pre-rat and post-rat. I suspect he sighed with relief when he caught the intruder. At least I hope he did. The curious thing was that following this announcement many of his friends "liked" his new status.

Another person described her status thus. *"What a glorious day! Days like this make me feel thankful that I am alive. To celebrate this I went for a walk with my cat."* The chronicle is not clear whether the feline was tethered or whether she enjoyed the walk snuggled in the crook of the owner's arm.

I get intimations from LinkedIn, Hotels.com, and most annoyingly from Fragrance Net. They have a perennial sale. They desperately want me to buy Oil of Olay because it is good for my skin. They offer me massive discounts. I am not sure how or why these people think that I have epidermal issues.

The most interesting is from a site called Twoo. It basically contains requests from octogenarian and septuagenarian ladies, who want to talk to me, develop a friendship, leading to a "meaningful relationship". I suppose it means tying the knot. Looking for men in their seventies. Of course, that disqualifies me right away. Also I don't play bingo, go to the Legion for an afternoon drink, dance or play pinochle.

Two letters are from friends.

But the fact that a friend's name appears does not guarantee that the mail is valid. Sometime ago I got a letter from a colleague and dear friend since 1972. I was quite excited to know what he had to say, especially since he had emigrated to the west coast, and the last intimation I had from him was that after 8 months, many boxes were yet to be opened. Anyway a great surprise was in store for me. He appeared to be peddling in Viagra! Granted we had discussed many themes during our very long association, but my libido was never a subject that came up. So I called him to find out what was happening and he told me that he was not moonlighting, that someone had hacked into my account, and I had better change my email address or at least my password, pronto.

I am sure that this is not an annoyance unique to me. We all are slaves to our email, to a certain extent. Recent studies show that office workers spend almost a third of their total workday reading and responding to messages. Psychologists say that this constant connectivity can be harmful. They have established a clear link between spending time on email and stress.

In her excellent book **Unsubscribe**, Jocelyn Glei posits that even though we may not care for the content of every email we receive, many of us are addicted to the act of checking email. It activates a primal impulse in our brains to seek out what behavioral psychologists call "random rewards".

Glei explains. "Imagine that email is like a slot machine. Most of the time when you 'pull the lever' to check your email messages, you get something disappointing or bothersome – a communication from a frustrated client or a boss with an urgent request. But every once in a while you get something exciting – email from a long lost friend, a flattering request to speak at a conference, announcement of the arrival of nephew… And it's those random rewards, mixed in with all mind numbing updates and irksome requests that we find so addictive. They want us to check our email again and again, even when we have better things to do."

I have a notion, possibly erroneous, that I have to clear all inbox entries so as not to clutter up the computer, and so I routinely strive for an empty inbox. Just when I think that the task is complete, a new message rolls in! And then another, this time from Justin Trudeau asking for money. And then there are those letters that require or even demand a response. How many times have I written, "Dear…, I am sorry that this response is late in coming…"

TATTOO CONVENTION

*(The pictures in this article were taken by photo journalist Felix Clay of **The Guardian**, London.)*

I had often toyed with the idea of getting a tattoo somewhere on my body. The *raison d'être* was, like everyone else sporting tattoos, to make a statement—preferably against society in general or an individual like Assad, Trump or Mugabe. Or so I thought.

I was wrong.

People disfigure their body for a variety of reasons! This came to light (at least for me) when I read about The International London Tattoo Convention which was held in London two years ago. Only then I realized that this convention was an annual event.

And you thought that conventions are only held for teachers, doctors, engineers, Shriners and such!

The 2016 convention was also a celebration of ten years of its existence. Over 400 of the world's finest, most famous, truly unique tattoo artists congregated at the vast, picturesque setting of Tobacco Dock, London. More than 20,000 people attended. The tattoo artists came from all over the world—Poland, Austria, Australia and the US, to name a few. The total attendance figures are not known yet, but last year more than 20,000 people attended. The visitors were able to watch these artists perform on the bodies of clients who were willing to pay exorbitant prices. The more complex the design, the more they paid. Also some of the artists were more in demand than others. Naturally.

These people are called artists because what they produce is truly artistic. But I would have preferred them working on a canvas rather than the derriere of men and women!

What is incredible to me was the reason some of the clients had in getting their bodies tattooed. Jysyna Derj of Yorkshire said that, "I find plain skin boring and feel ashamed of the empty spaces on my body." And just look at these other examples:

Lee Risvik of Norway said, "There is no meaning
behind it...It's just beautiful and cool."

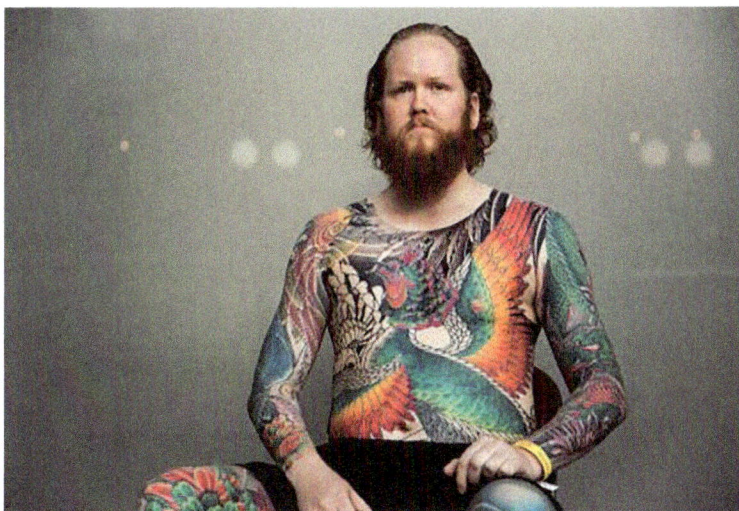

You will notice that Mr Nisvik no longer needs to invest in a shirt.

Mr Makinen of Finland is more philosophical about the whole thing. He says that the "Tattoos are a reflection of how I see myself within. They are like an ongoing diary."

Some diary!! I believe you, pal, I really do. But I would be nervous confronting you in a dark alley.

If Mr. Nisvik no longer needs a shirt, the unnamed man on the right in the picture below needs only a codpiece in his wardrobe.

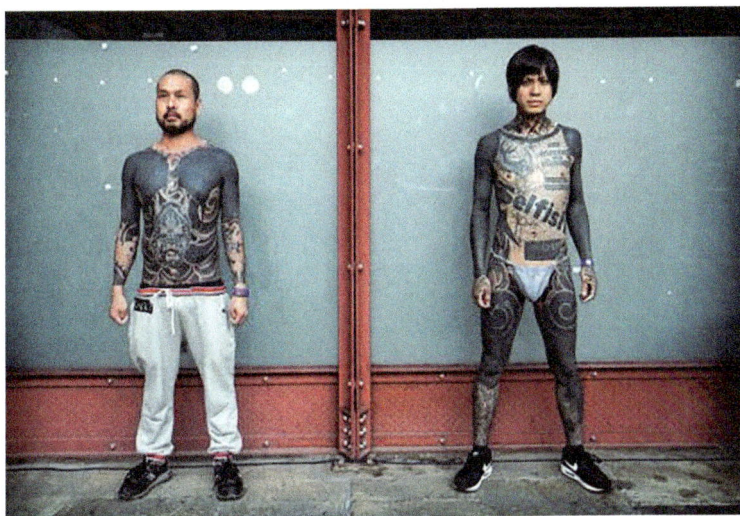

I am not sure what he does in real life for a living. Would he appear for a job interview dressed in a tattoo?

"According to a recent survey a fifth of all British adults have been inked. Among 16 to 44 year olds, both men and women, the figure rises to 29%." says Felix Clay who has provided a photo gallery of the convention. He continues, "In the US, where an estimated 40% of households have at least one member who has a tattoo."

I have given below a few of the entrants at the London Festival.

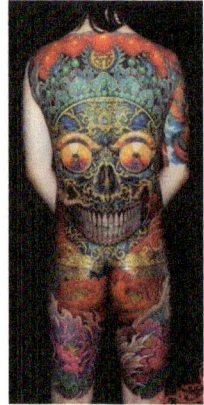

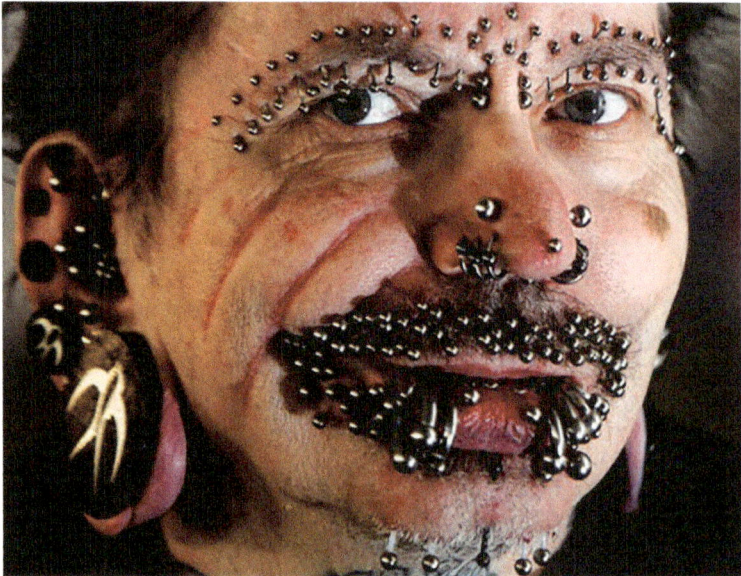

Not an example of tattoos, but I imagine most of you have never seen (and will never see again) anything like this and so I had to share it!

FIESTAS

I am not sure what the primitive man did for relaxation. Arguably his days entailed hard work. After all, killing a mastodon without proper weapons would have been a mighty task. Then skinning the beast would have been even harder. So how did he relax after the toil during the day? Perhaps he met with neighbors and swapped hunting stories, discussed the need for sharper tools. We don't know.

The ancient Greeks had many diversions. There was always a play to go to. Or they could run the marathon or chuck the javelin or the discus. And of course, there was the army. The Greeks were perennially at war with whoever was available. More often than not, the cause of war would have been to establish territorial imperatives. Or, of course, they abducted the neighboring king's wife. Retrieving the woman sometimes took years, ten to be exact in the case of Helen of Troy.

The Romans too had many diversions. A fairly innocuous event was the chariot race in the various colosseums around the country. In major centres they had gladiator schools, where beefy slaves were trained to fight to the death. We all have seen in the movies the vanquished slave lying on the ground bleeding, the victor waiting for the signal (thumbs down) from the royalty (in most cases the queen) to kill. On special occasions the slaves (who were Christians) were made to fight hungry lions, and inevitably the lion was the victor (except in the case of Androcles where, in a gesture of *quid pro quo*, the lion let him go).

During medieval times, when the knights were not busy saving damsels in distress, they engaged themselves in jousting and the people gathered to watch. The Spaniards congregated in round arenas and watched the matador kill enraged bulls. This was more or less a year round activity.

But over the centuries the people became more civilized and hence organized their festivities around religious and social events. That includes the Spaniards. They came up with a strange ritual every year to celebrate the San Fermin Festival from the 6th to the 14th of July. It is called the **Pamplona Bull Run**. In this curious form of entertainment, six bulls already earmarked for the bull ring in the afternoon (and hence horrendously abused and made angry), are let loose on a narrow pathway and allowed to chase participants who run to avoid being gored (see picture on next page).

Image credit: Reuters

About 25,000 people participate in this 'sport'. The objective is to avoid the chasing bull. The length of the run is 825 metres. The bulls eventually end up in the arena to face a matador. People have been known to get gored to death during the run.

If this sounds a curious form of entertainment, they get 'curiouser'. If you happen to be in the village of Bunol, Italy, on the last Wednesday in August, you can join over 20,000 people in the **Tomatina Street Festival** (see pictures on next page). Participants collect as many ripe tomatoes as possible and for an hour engage themselves in throwing the fruits at one another.

Image credit: Latomatina.org

On the 31st of August in 2016 trucks dumped 150 tons of tomatoes! Whether the unused tomatoes eventually ended up in the Heinz bottles as ketchup or not, I am not sure!

But the craziest of all these diversions is the **Italian International Highline Meeting Festival**. Participants from all over the world gather to socialize, take yoga lessons and such. When it is time for a shut eye, they go to their own hammocks, except that they are strung hundreds of feet high on tight ropes anchored on the peaks of the Italian Alps.

Many countries have unusual festivals. The Indians celebrate **Holi**, the festival of colors on the full moon day in February/early March. To celebrate the arrival of spring and also the victory of good over evil, people gather on the streets and throw colored water at one another. Powder is also used.

Agit Agueda Art Festival in Portugal, which was started in 2006, makes an unparalleled contribution to the cultural landscape of the city. Over 500 music groups perform during a week of celebrations. But the installation of thousands of colored umbrellas over the city's streets is the highlight of the festival.

Image credit: Patricia Almeida

A SPADE BY ANY OTHER NAME

I don't know if you have noticed; you can't buy razors any more. You have to shop for a **shaving system**. I have one: the Gillette Fusion shaving system. (Yes, I do shave!)

Like the razor, supervisors are a dying breed; they are being replaced by **facilitators**. And employees are morphing into **associates**.

While these Darwinian events are intelligible and perhaps acceptable, the stuff that comes out of the computer technology world simply boggles the mind. A California based software outfit once advertised one of their products thus: **The WebTop is a new, innovative browser- based interface that allows server-based applications and server administration functions to be securely accessed from a browser.**

Well, pal, I believe you! I will take your word for it.

Or how about this memo someone wrote? **"John, do you think we should call an off-site to discuss next month's deliverables? That way, we can identify any disconnects and forward an action plan to the impacted sales reps."**

Excuse me, what did you say?

Now, going back to shaving systems, facilitators and such, you will find euphemistic uses in other fields as well. You can't buy **used cars** anymore; you get **pre-owned cars**. Physicians are starting to call stimulant drugs **activity boosters**. Mechanics are **automotive internists**. Pre-schoolers are enrolled in **early learning centres**, where they wander around between **pupil stations** which were, in my school days, called desks. And ah, the library! That room with the musty odour, where the ominous legend "SILENCE" cowed you into submission is in a state of RIP. They are being replaced by **learning resource centres**. If your little guy brings a report card which says that *"Johnny has the ability to channel his hyper energy into activities inside and outside the class room."* it means that the blighter revels in pulling girls' pig tails and bullying kids in general.

And if you step into the political world of the United States, you would notice that euphemism gets royal treatment. For instance there is no **torture** in their vocabulary, but only **enhanced interrogation techniques**. And their politicians don't ever tell lies; they occasionally **misspeak**.

We use euphemistic statements when dealing with subjects that are personal, sensitive or not quite *correct*. Thus people **pass away** or **meet their maker** or perhaps **kick the bucket**. We **put an animal out of its misery**. Toilets or urinals are no longer, having been replaced by washrooms and restrooms. I am still struggling to find any logic in calling ladies' spaces **powder rooms** and why women need to powder just their noses, and not the other parts of their face. And the portals of these invaluable spaces do not anymore display 'gentlemen' or 'ladies'. Instead, we find abstract and often obtuse drawings which sometimes confuse patrons. I admit that it has confused me on more than one occasion.

But there are many misleading euphemisms. **Between jobs** actually means unemployed. **Binocular deprivation** is not what it sounds. It is sewing the animal's eyes shut for purposes of research. **Bio solids** are sewage sludge. **Ethnic cleansing** is a poor attempt at a civilized term for genocide.

Personally though, I stay away from such use. In my no-nonsense household if I asked for grub, I will get just that – a caterpillar! And I am not called a senior citizen but an old goat. That is calling a spade a spade!

MIDDLING IT

I am not quite certain who invented the name **John Q Public**. But I do know that the moniker would lose its charm if 'Q' is substituted with another letter of the alphabet. "R' would be harsh; 'B' would be, well blah!

I am not also sure what 'Q' stands for. Usually it is the first letter of the middle name. It could not be Quatezalcoatl because it is Aztec. Possibly Quinn, a very Irish name. By the way, for the benefit of my fans in far flung climes, John Q Public is a term used to denote a hypothetical member of society deemed a 'common man', a selected 'man on the street'. He must not be a criminal, though. If he is, the name changes to 'perp', short form of perpetrator.

Compounding my ignorance even further, I don't know why people ever use the middle initial. There is a school of thought that claims that a middle initial can actually increase others' perceptions of your intelligence. Two initials give you gravitas. This theory is posited by psychologists Wijinand A.P. Tilburg and Eric R. Igou of the University of Limerick, Ireland. I don't want to belabor you with the details of the research. Please accept my word for it.

According to Bruce Feiler the middle initial is actually a recent invention. Middle names first began to appear in Europe in the late Middle Ages, but they weren't widely used until the 19th century, when populations boomed and people needed more names to distinguish themselves. Middle initials became ubiquitous in the 20th century. Several US Presidents used them. But we also find that many famous people are known by their middle name. George **Orson** Welles, Thomas **Sean** Connery and William **Somerset** Maugham come to mind.

We are, of course, saddled with the names our parents give us at the time of birth. Elsewhere I made a mention of Kim Kardashian's daughter who is called North West! In India, however, only certain communities seem to use a middle name, which is usually the name of the father. Most people on the west coast seem to use a middle name. Perhaps in the most famous name coming out of west India is M.K. Gandhi; 'K' stands for the name of his father, his given name being Mohandas.

In the eastern and northern parts of India, people generally don't use the middle name at all. Rabindranath Tagore, for instance, hailed from Bengal. But in the state where I come from, it seems that the norms don't apply. For a vast majority of us, the first name is the father's name, the given name is in the middle and the last name is, well, last. Thus my official name is Parameswaran Sukumar Nayar. Which is okay in my home state. But when I emigrated to Africa, the people assumed that the name that appears first was the given name, and addressed me as Parameswaran though it was actually my father's name. Even today, I get letters from banks and other institutions addressing me as 'Dear Parameswaran'! Receptionists get tongue tied. A few them apologize because they know that they have mutilated my name. But I am very generous. I end up apologizing and tell them that I wish my name were John Smith or Bill Fletcher or Bob Tannas!

The difficulty comes when you have to fill out forms – applying for a credit card, for instance – where space is limited. But then I suppose I should thank the Lord for small mercies, and be happy that I was not born in Sri Lanka. I can't imagine how Mr Herath, a well-known cricketer, manages his name: Mudiyan Selage Rangana Keerthi Bandara Herath! What exactly is his middle initial?

Another person who might have problems filling out application forms would be the Prince of Wales. His name is Charles Philip Arthur George. I am not sure what his middle initials are. Maybe he does not have to fill out forms, being the future king and all that.

P.S. – While the middle initial might be an indication of one's intelligence and the barometer of gravitas, in the general social set up we live in, the importance of the middle finger cannot be overestimated. Essentially, the longest digit of the hand is an important tool for effective communication. It has a vocabulary all its own. For those who overly depend on body language, the middle finger is very crucial. It is an essential tool to communicate raw emotions. Without it, one is virtually mute, as Obama observed when referring to his first Chief of Staff, Rahm Emmanuel, who lost his middle finger in an accident in the work shop.

HOW INSULTING! (1)

As we all know, before Donald Trump became the President, he had to compete with 21 others in a dog and pony show called the Primaries. Senators, Governors, Congressmen, a doctor, a dismissed business woman and Trump himself appeared on national television and instead of discussing policy and enlightening the people about what they would do if elected, they hurled insults at each other on stage.

Trump called Senator and war hero John McCain a dummy for finishing at the bottom of his class at the Naval Academy. He also said that all this chatter about McCain being a war hero is rubbish. Trump declared that McCain was being touted as a hero because he was captured. If he had not been, he would have been just another veteran. McCain's sidekick, Senator Lindsey Graham, said that Trump is a jackass. So Trump called Graham a lightweight and an idiot. Ex-Governor Rick Perry called Trump a cancer. Senator Marco Rubio said that President Obama has no class. He said, "Obama eats cereal out of a bathtub." Exactly what he meant by this is not clear—whether the President of the United States uses the bathtub instead of the cereal bowl or whether he has a perverse habit of eating breakfast in the tub (many people eat their breakfast in bed). Mike Huckabee said that Obama (by signing the deal with Iran) was marching Israelis to "the door of the oven"— a highly insensitive reference to the Holocaust. It is difficult to get a good read on these sentiments. Whether hurling insults at each other is a pre-requisite for getting votes is open to question. Beyond that, are they funny or tragic?

And why, indeed, do people insult others? Here psychologists are divided in their opinion. One school of thought argues that it is a show of power, that people insult others because they can. Others seem to think that insults are thrown by weaklings, since they don't have anything more potent with which to attack the enemy.

Insults are as old as history. It is, for example, reasonable to assume that Adam was pretty peeved when Eve did a number on him and made him eat the apple. I am not sure what language this couple used to communicate with each other. Perhaps Sumerian or a form of Hebrew.

Demosthenes, the story goes, had an altercation with Phocion, the Athenian statesman and said, "The Athenians will kill you, Phocion, if they go crazy." And Phocion responded, "But they will kill **you** if they come to their senses."

Cicero was very fond of using invective in the Senate, especially when talking about Mark Anthony, making veiled statements about him being homosexual. Anthony himself was a bisexual. We have his dalliance with Cleopatra as proof. Ask Bernard Shaw.

Shakespeare freely used insults. Mark how Prince Henry talks about Falstaff, "You clay-brained fatso, you knuckle-headed fools, you son of a whore, you obscene tub of lard....."

The 18th President of the United States, Ulysses S Grant, said this of the 20th President, Garfield. "Garfield has shown that he is not possessed of the backbone of a worm."

And H.L Mencken said of Calvin Coolidge, "He slept more than any President, whether by day or night. Nero fiddled, but Coolidge only snored."

Margaret Asquith, wife of Prime Minister Asquith, said of Winston Churchill, 'He would kill his own grandmother just so that he could use her skin to make a drum to beat his own praise."

Compared with these, the language used by Trump, Rubio, *et al* is nursery school stuff.

From the examples I have given above, one might tend to think that hurling insults is the prerogative of politicians. The prince of insults in the non-political sector happens to be a prince in real life—Prince Philip of the Realm. He has an uncanny ability to put his foot in his mouth.

When he turned 90 a few years ago, The Daily Mirror published 90 classic gaffes to celebrate his birthday... one for each year. Obviously I have no space to publish all 90, but here are a few classic clangers:

To the President of Nigeria who was in national dress, "You look like you're ready for bed." (see picture on the next page). Note the expression on the Prince's face!

To a British trekker in Papua New Guinea, "You managed not to get eaten then."

To a British student in China, "If you stay here much longer, you'll go home with slitty eyes."

HOW INSULTING! (2)

The previous article basically dealt with verbal insults hurled by people at one another. I also suggested that this malaise is more rampant among politicians. One does not hear Bill Gates employing derogatory language against Warren Buffet for instance. Federer is unlikely to insult Nadal in public.

Insults need not necessarily be verbal. Michael Argyle in his book **The Psychology of Interpersonal Behavior** suggests that humans have more than 700,000 forms of body language! Somewhat difficult to believe, but I have no means with which to argue with Argyle. It is only natural that some of the movements would be employed to show displeasure or to insult others.

Even though we all may not speak the same language, some of the usages of body language are more or less universal. When people are happy, you can see it in their body language, especially from the expression on their face and sometimes from the way they walk. Some nonverbal insults are just as easy to understand. When trying to communicate with someone, you can tell if the person is upset with you just by the way he or she looks at you. They could be smiling, but you know if it is fake and you know instinctively whether they are simply pushing themselves to smile for whatever reason.

Having said that, a given gesture does not convey the same meaning everywhere. Ask George W. Bush. When he was visiting Australia in 1992, from the window of his limousine he held up his index and middle fingers in the "V" shape a *la* Winston Churchill. This means victory in England or peace in North America. George, whose knowledge about these things is sketchy at best, flashed the 'V' sign backwards, with the back of his hand facing the people. The next day his photo appeared in newspapers across Australia with the headline, **President Bush Insults Australians.** He was unaware that the 'reverse' sign is an obscene gesture! It is tantamount to giving the middle finger.

This disparity in body language causes untold difficulties for people who travel. This is because there is no globally acceptable non-verbal communication grammar. Take handshakes for example. While handshakes are generally accepted as a form of greeting in many cultures, the acceptance depends a lot on how much pressure you use during the process. The length of time you keep your hands locked also means different things in different cultures. If someone in Latin America withdraws their hand quickly, you can be sure you have insulted the person. In Nigeria 'thumbs up' is an insulting gesture. In Russia do not—repeat do not—give anyone the 'OK' sign with the thumb and the forefinger forming the letter 'O'. I know. I did it once; just once and never again. It means in what English vernacular is the rear orifice of a donkey.

"Smile and the whole world smiles with you." Or so goes the saying. But be careful how you employ it in Asian countries. Smiling at a person you don't know is simply unacceptable, especially if you are smiling at a woman. If the woman is accompanied by a male escort, you might be in real trouble. Public displays of affection are frowned upon in many countries. Using your left hand to touch or eat is unacceptable in many cultures. In many countries in Asia, the Middle East and Africa food is offered communally, meaning people sit around the food and grab it with their right hand. The left hand is considered unclean.

The feet are also considered unclean. If you don't have any footwear on, your feet can get filthy. Ergo, in the Middle East it is highly insulting to show the sole of one's foot or shoe to someone. This causes a cultural problem because we are prone to cross our legs while sitting around in a living room, for instance. Next time you see the photographs of dignitaries sitting with Arab leaders, watch for this. You will find that the feet of the visitors are firmly planted on the ground.

The ultimate show of displeasure in Arab Countries is throwing the shoe at someone. In 2007, Iraqi journalist Muntadhar al-Zaidi threw his shoe at President Bush during a press conference (see picture on next page).

When it happened, many in the west did not understand the deeper significance.

The Darker Side

THE DARKER SIDE

The tenor of the articles thus far has been one of levity, even though some of the themes could lend themselves to serious treatment. The world around us is in such a state of turmoil that events around us do not necessarily make us chuckle. As the poet Dowson said, "They are not long, the days of wine and roses." Unpleasant and uncomfortable elements assault our sensibilities and clamor for our attention every day.

Literati classify events as 'tragic' or 'comedic'. But truly tragic events in Greek terms tell us the story of the fall of mighty men like Agamemnon or Macbeth. Such tragedies are not common, though today we all agree that some events, namely the Holocaust, are tragic. Natural calamities like the tsunami and earthquakes which cause widespread death and destruction are tragic. Stoning a woman to death who has (allegedly) insulted the Quran is tragic. Beheading foreign reporters, for whatever reason, is tragic.

Every day we get reports of events that are best classified as unpleasant. If you are the President of the US and during a press conference someone decides to throw a shoe at you, it cannot be considered pleasant. Bernard Shaw did not write 'tragedies' like Shakespeare. He was reluctant to call **Caesar and Cleopatra** a tragedy. He preferred to categorize his works as "plays pleasant" and "plays unpleasant".

I have included five articles in this section—tragic, unpleasant or both.

TORTURE

Lord Acton (1839-1902) is credited with the now rather clichéd expression, "Power corrupts, but absolute power corrupts absolutely." Who Lord Acton was or when and why he said this is irrelevant. The fact is that the essence of the statement was true in the past, and it is still true today, especially when those in power employ torture for gathering information or for punitive purposes.

The Greeks, for instance, had many ingenious ways of torturing people, ranging from the delicate to the brutal. King Xerxes used to banish criminals to the **Island of Perpetual Tickling** where the victim would be continuously tickled with a large feather by a relay team of soldiers, and the victim would laugh until he/she died. You have of course, heard the expression *'tickled to death'*. The Greeks also invented the Brazen Bull (see picture on next page).

It was a solid piece of brass which was cast with a door on one side that could be opened and latched. The victim would be placed inside the bull and a fire set underneath it until the metal became literally yellow.

Medieval forms of torture are well known. The mid twentieth century saw an Austrian corporal who capitalized on Germany's high inflation become Chancellor and massacre six million Jews because he said they were *untermenschen* (subhuman). He wanted Germany to be 'pure'. It was a country meant for Aryans only. Ethnic cleansing in Europe, mass genocide in Africa… the examples are numerous.

All these atrocities were committed by people who had the power to do it. Over the last two decades we have heard of people employing torture to elicit information in the name of national security. Prisoners are incarcerated in jails, Guantanamo being one of the most notorious. Prisoners there were routinely subjected to waterboarding, which simulates drowning. Dick Cheney, George W's VP, would swear on the Bible or the Torah that it was not torture; it was just an innocuous method of interrogation.

Using water cannons and tear gas canisters to disperse unruly crowds are routinely employed in many countries.

Sometimes soldiers are ordered to use rubber bullets to deal with surging crowds. An uncooperative perpetrator is sometimes subjected to pepper spray on the face. Ouch!

And those in power are constantly seeking new and original means of crowd control. There is unrest everywhere in the world, and Israel is no exception. The government constantly has to deal with unruly Palestinians.

Enter Odor Tech.

This is an outfit that specializes in the research and development of advanced non-toxic, non-lethal scent-based repellents for law enforcement. And they have come up with a foul smelling liquid called 'skunk'.

Your first reaction would be related to the mammal called skunk. Of all the fauna in the world, the skunk got a rough deal. It does not have defence mechanisms like a hard shell (tortoise) or spikes (porcupine) or horns. But it has two powerful anal scent glands which produce a foul smelling fluid which the mammal sprays at the enemy. Those who have encountered a skunk would recall that it is somewhat difficult to remove the stench from the clothes or the body for that matter.

Odor Tech's 'skunk' is, as I mentioned above, a fluid which is dispersed as a form of a yellow mist. This product was developed for the use of the **Israel Defence Forces (IDF)** for mob control. Israel claims that it is an improvement on tear gas and rubber bullets.

A BBC reporter describes its effects as follows. "Imagine the worst foul thing you have ever smelled. An overpowering mix of rotting meat, old socks that have not been washed for weeks – topped off with the pungent waft of an open sewer– imagine being covered in the stuff as it is liberally sprayed from a water cannon.

Then imagine not being able to get rid of the stench for at least three days, no matter how often you scrub yourself clean."

To further punish the protesters the IDF sometimes drive up to the Palestinian settlements and spray the houses.

The behavior of Xerxes, Adolf, Cheney and now Netanyahu exemplifies the abuse of power. The populace is helpless.

The stuff has found its way into the United States. Baltimore, Kentucky and St. Louis have already a stockpile.

VLADIMIR (1)

In August 2001, I was sent on assignment to a city in Russia called Vladimir. The city has a very large Jewish community. The Jewish Cultural Center is called **Hesed Lev** and they got a grant from UNESCO, in response to their request for funds to promote Jewish culture through the performing arts. Many Jews had been killed during the Soviet regime beginning with Stalin, and the younger generation in Russia was growing up without any knowledge of or sensitivity to their rich heritage. **Hesed Lev** wanted to tour the country to promote Jewish culture with a variety show including plays, dances and folk songs. The grant would help underwrite the expenses, but they wanted someone to put a program together and organize a "Festival", which could be taken on the road. I was assigned this task.

Needless to say I was quite excited. The members of the Center were excited as well. I was asked to accept room and board with one of the staff, Katrina, and I agreed. They could not afford to waste precious dollars on hotel accommodations, three course meals and such! I agreed.

Finalizing the program, rehearsing the individual items, planning the tour etc. were quite fascinating. The enthusiasm of the cast and crew was exhilarating. The cast that was rehearsing Fiddler on the Roof were thrilled that I was part of the show in Grande Prairie.

One day my hostess Katrina asked me if I would agree to meet her grandfather Professor Roid Dubov. His parents had been political prisoners during the Soviet Regime. He had a Ph.D. in geophysics and a D.Sc. in geological chemistry. He was one of the most respected scientists in Russia. He was also an internationally known geologist. He spoke English in a fashion.

I asked Katrina if he would care to talk about his traumatic experiences. She said that normally he did not, but she was sure he would make an exception in my case. I told her to warn him that I might pry!

The deep furrows on a prematurely aged face bore eloquent testimony to a life of pain, harsh memories, trauma and anger. The tall frame was gaunt; the gait was slow but dignified. The brown eyes had a fierce glint and the profile was strangely reminiscent of actor Rex Harrison.

His wife, Susanna had a typical Russian dinner all laid out in the living room. They did not have a dining room. Meals were usually taken in the kitchen. His daughter Aksana, a professor of English at the Vladimir Polytechnic, also was present.

"My English is not very good. No chance to practise. But if you stay with me for a month, it will come back," he said with a chuckle. "But Aksana helps."

"You are doing all right," I said to encourage him.

"I have been to Canada. Very friendly people. The Rockies fascinated me. Banff is so beautiful. We don't have anything like that in Russia. I was the key note speaker at an international conference of geologists. This was in Ottawa 25 years ago. Of course, I had an interpreter."

He excused himself and brought a bound edition of the proceedings of the conference. He showed me his contribution. His picture twenty five years before showed a very handsome man.

He started to share his story. He said his father was arrested before his eyes by 12 soldiers wielding machine guns. A few days later they came for his mother.

He was ten years old. But he had clear memories of the day… how his mother cried, how the soldiers roughed her up. A few months later he would learn that his father was executed. His mother was not killed, only because she was a robust, good looking woman. One cannot imagine what happened to her in the concentration camps in Siberia.

"I was offered a job by the Canadian government," he said. "But I chose to return to Russia. This is my homeland." A cloud passed over his face and after a brief moment of introspection he added, "Yes. This is home, whatever happened."

"But you have bitter memories," I said, catching the moment. I had been wondering how to broach the subject.

"Yes, I do."

"But what crimes did they commit? What were they accused of?"

"This is bizarre," he said with help from Aksana. "My father was the chief engineer of S.E. Railways; he was a highly placed official."

His deputy was jealous of him. Knowing that Dr. Dubov Sr. would be at the helm of affairs for a long time, and having his own eye on the job, his deputy regularly fed stories to the party officials saying that Dr. Dubov Sr. was not a Bolshevik and had clear anti-communist views. This went on for several months. One Sunday morning, the soldiers walked in and arrested him. His mother was picked up a few days later. What crimes she had committed was not explained.

They were sent to separate camps. After 10 years, his mother was transferred to another camp because she had contracted gonorrhea. During the transfer she managed to let fly out of the train window a letter with details about where she had been and where she was going.

"It was a miracle that someone picked the letter up and took it to my grandfather," Dubov continued. "I grew up with my grandfather. I was 24 when I saw my mother again."

There was no emotion when he described the scene. "I had always remembered her as a very beautiful woman… full breasted, with large piercing eyes. But what the soldiers brought back was a gaunt, skinny woman. Her bones were sticking out. She was almost bald. The large blue eyes were in some sunken hole on the face. At first, I was not prepared to accept that she was my mother. Then she cried out, 'Roey!' And I burst out crying. She died two years later." The eyes wandered again…painful images.

Time for toasts. The first of many is, "welcome to the guest and to peace in the world".

I asked, "Do you feel uncomfortable talking about those days?" He said, "It was difficult in the beginning. Now I don't mind. I talk about this only to special people." he said. I was very touched.

"It is a great thing you are doing," he continued. "**Hesed Lev** is doing a great job trying to promote Jewish culture and the Jewish tradition. One does not realize how easy it is to destroy and how difficult it is to rebuild. The Soviets broke the backbone of the Russian Jews."

I mumbled something by way of gratitude.

"It has been an honor," he said. "I wish I could speak better English. Will you come again?"

"I'll try," I said.

But I did not go again. I could not. I had met the Dubovs on the 6th of September. In three days, the World Trade Center was demolished and I was repatriated in a hurry.

The meeting with Dr. Dubov is an indelible memory.

VLADIMIR (2)

16 of January 1989 was an important day in the history of the erstwhile Czechoslovakia. On this day Vaclav Havel, playwright and political activist, was inaugurated as the first democratically elected President, thus toppling the communist government backed by the Soviet Union.

The interesting fact is that Havel, along with many activists including students and journalists, was in a jail in Bratislava on the day he was elected.

A few days before my visit with Dr. Dubov on the 6th of September 2001, I got a surprise call from Alexander Sergeev of the Russia desk in Moscow. He had a request from UNESCO. Three Israelis would be arriving in Vladimir on the 7th of September. They were journalists who wrote articles of protest against the Russian occupation of Czechoslovakia. At that time they were operating independently from Moscow, Odessa and Kiev for different news organizations. They were arrested and sent to Vladimir central prison, which is the largest in Russia. It was (and perhaps still is) the most notorious prison in the country and the most dangerous criminals or those who needed to be 'taught a lesson' were sent there.

The three men spent about six years or so in the jail and when Czechoslovakia became a democratic republic, they were released. They moved to Israel. But they were returning to Vladimir after many years to see the prison where they had been incarcerated, where they withstood indescribable torture, but survived simply because of their indomitable spirit.

I was the only UN presence in Vladimir and so I was requested to interview them and submit a report. I arranged for a meeting on the 11 of September.

Yes, 9/11!!

The journalists – Benyamin, Isaac and Menachem – had horror stories to tell. One particularly cruel treatment is worth mentioning because you, perhaps, have not heard about it. Every Friday was 'silence' day. From 5 in the morning when they were up until 5 a.m. the next day, the prisoners in their ward were not allowed to make any sound. Food was served on paper plates, the toilet was not to be flushed, and if anyone felt like sneezing, he had to stifle it. Isaac said that was the most brutal in the Russian repertoire of torture.

To listen to the three people describe their experiences was extremely disturbing. I had to ask them why, in God's name, they came back to Vladimir! They said that they wanted to see once more the place where they had fought the brutal machinery of the KGB and beaten it. They were writing a book, describing their experiences, and they wanted to see the city which they had not had the opportunity to explore, having spent all the time in prison. As I said they were incarcerated for six years and when Czechoslovakia became independent, they were sent from Vladimir to Haifa.

What happened to me on September 11 is material for another article. But I will say this. On the 12th I was whisked out of Vladimir in great secrecy, under escort and sent back to Canada that very day, by the most indirect route possible!

Though the three Israelis and I exchanged addresses and promised to communicate regularly, alas, it has not happened. I have no idea where they are in Israel. I am not even sure if they are still alive. However, once in a while I think of my conversation with the three gentlemen and shudder at the extent to which man can inflict pain on another human being.

Since I had to be evacuated from Russia in a hurry, I could not stay until the project for which I was hired was complete. Alexander told me that the troupe did, indeed, visit Moscow to put on a show. Whether they traveled widely in Russia or not, he was not sure.

IS KILLING A SPORT?

It is reasonable to assume that you pilgrims have at some time or the other experienced pain. I recall that my father caned me once for entering the house without washing my feet. I was away playing hopscotch with friends. In primary school, teachers also caned me for not showing any signs of mastering the arithmetic tables. Caning hurts, I tell you! Who has not stubbed a toe, or had a headache? Many of us have suffered people who are acknowledged to be a pain in the derriere. Labor pain, pain due to cancer or arthritis and the mother of all pains, the fearsome root canal…the list is endless.

It is reasonable to assume also that animals feel pain, though I believe it is hard to prove. Of course, a dog yelps when hit with a stick. We see jockeys using a whip to coax the horse to run faster. But the buffalo who gets routinely hit when the speed with which it pulls the plough is not acceptable suffers the pain without any outward exhibition of its effect.

Primitive man hunted to secure food for him and his family. But killing the animals just for the fun of it is a curse of modern civilization. It certainly is not fun for the animal being hunted. Ask the foxes in Great Britain. The poor animal is chased by a bunch of drunken gentry on horseback, assisted by a pack of dogs. Oscar Wilde described it best, "The English country gentleman galloping after a fox—the unspeakable in full pursuit of the uneatable."

Gentleman? Forsooth!!

The hunting of wild animals is considered a sport. To refresh my memory I just now looked up the meaning of the word. Webster declares, "An athletic activity requiring skill or physical prowess and often of a competitive nature, as racing, baseball, tennis, golf, boxing, fishing etc." I am not sure if the "etc." is supposed to include hunting of defenceless animals. Probably.

Be that as it may, the actions two years ago of a dentist in Minnesota, Dr. Walter Palmer, had generated a lot of outrage by his *'sporting'* activities. In early July 2016, he went to Zimbabwe and killed a lion. This, as such, should not have caused any commotion. After all he claimed to be a professional hunter. He routinely went to Africa and killed wild animals. In fact, he killed a lion in 2008 (see picture on next page). Note the happiness, the satisfaction on his mug!! Palmer is the guy on the left, by the way.

In 2016 he was after a special lion, which incidentally had a name—Cecil. He was a protected animal. He was the subject of a study by Oxford University researchers. He had a collar around his neck so that the researchers could track his whereabouts. He had a majestic mane.

To achieve his goal Palmer paid $50,000 to two Zimbabweans who used bait to lure the 13 year old animal out of a national park, where Cecil was protected, into territory where lion hunting was legal. There Palmer wounded the animal with an arrow, and then stalked him for nearly two days before killing him with a rifle, decapitating and skinning him and leaving the carcass to rot in the sun. For over 40 hours the animal must have experienced agonizing pain.

There was universal outcry at the heinous act by the good doctor, but he played the innocent victim. He issued the following statement. "I deeply regret that my pursuit of an activity that I love and practise responsibly and legally resulted in the taking of this lion."

An activity that you *love?* Seriously, Walter? You *love* seeking out and killing something regal and beautiful? If so what is the difference between you and the ISIS thugs who routinely deface and demolish World Heritage Sites?

There is another thing that he loves. Women. Not just their teeth, but other parts of their anatomy. In 2009 he settled sexual harassment allegations by a former employee who was also his patient. He doled out $127,000 in settlements.

Palmer had violated laws in the US and in Zimbabwe and if the Africans demanded it, he could have been extradited. I hoped he was. I hoped that while in the prison he developed tooth ache. I hoped the dentist recommended a root canal. I hoped he got the root canal treatment without anesthetic.

Across the world, news media and social media had reported the outrage felt by people at this callous incident. But nothing was more poignant than the reaction from ten year old Piper Hoppe. She sat on the steps of Palmer's clinic with a poster which said, "Dr. Palmer, why did you kill Cecil?"

Why, indeed?

THE MOVING FINGER WRITES...

A Dutch couple had been saving for their dream holiday – a trip to Bali. They were looking forward to seeing the obligatory Kecak dance, Ramayana ballet, shadow theatre and such, but they were most interested in attending a Balinese funeral. And they were so disappointed that they could not, because nobody nearby died during the week they were there! They tried to take the hotel to task for false advertising because, it appears that one of the attractions the hotel offered was a funeral.

I can't blame them, because the Balinese funeral is unique. I had occasion to participate in one, mostly because I stayed in Bali for 4 months in connection with my post-grad research, and there were a few deaths reported during that period. Unlike in many cultures, the Balinese funeral is a happy occasion. It is considered a rite of passage. It is a big send-off for the soul, which departs leaving the body behind. Balinese are ancestor worshippers and as such they ensure that the ancestors are taken care of. So a typical funeral consists of a very elaborate procession. The dead body is carried on a high palanquin (litter), the community following the pall bearers dancing and singing until they reach the burial ground. After the cremation, a feast is served for all participants, an effort not too taxing for the family concerned because it is a huge pot luck affair.

This report of the Dutch couple and the Balinese ritual inspired me to consider the views on death by thinkers and poets in other cultures.

One of my earliest recollections is a poem by a relatively unknown poet of the 17 century, **John Shirley**. He said that death is a leveller:

> "The glories of our blood and state,
> Are shadows, not substantial things;
> There is no armour against fate,
> Death lays its icy hand on kings.
> Sceptre and crown must tumble down,
> And in the dust be equal made
> With the poor crooked scythe and spade."

While Shirley suggests the inevitability of death, others are not so meek and naïve. **John Dunne**, for instance, almost challenged death and disparaged it. He wrote:

> "Death, be not proud, though some have called thee
> Mighty and dreadful, for thou are not so...
> x x x x
> One short sleep past we wake eternally,

And Death shall be no more; Death thou shalt die."

Another man who had scant respect for death was **Dylan Thomas**. He saw man locked in a round of identities – with the beginning of growth as the first movement towards death, the first beginnings of love leading to procreation, new growth and so, in turn, to death again. He ridiculed death. He said that, "Death shall have no dominion."

The Balinese are not afraid of death. **Julius Caesar** wasn't either. When Calpurnia, his wife, did not like the news that the priests brought, prior to his historic trip to the Senate, she entreated him to stay home. Being a great soldier, he could not allow his decisions to be influenced by fear of death. So he said, "Of all the wonders that I yet have heard, it seems to me most strange that men should fear, seeing that death, a necessary end, will come when it will come."

Omar Khayyam, the 11 century Persian poet, perhaps, expresses the above sentiment most beautifully.

> "The moving finger writes; and having Writ
> Moves on: nor all thy Piety nor Wit
> Shall lure it back to cancel half a line
> Nor all the tears wash out a Word of it."

To conclude this, I could not find anything more exquisite than one of the stanzas from Gitanjali by Indian poet

Rabindranath Tagore who won the Nobel Prize for literature in the early 20thh century.

"I know the day will come when my sight shall be lost, and life will

Take its leave in silence, drawing the last curtain over my eyes.

Yet, stars will watch at night, and morning rise as before and hours

Heave like sea waves, drawing the last curtain over my eyes.

When I think of this end of my moments, the barrier of the moments

Breaks and I see by the light of death thy world with its careless treasures.

Rare is its lowest seat, rare is its meanest of lives.

Things I longed for in vain that I got—let them pass.

Let me but truly possess the things I spurned and overlooked.

AND EVERY SINGLE ONE
WAS SOMEONE

The book is called **And Every Single One Was Someone**. It has 1,250 pages. It is 8.5" wide and 11.5" long. It weighs 7.4 pounds and as such it is not the usual coffee table book. The book has no narrative, no plot, no texts or subtexts. There is not even a title on the cover, which instead features a Jewish prayer shawl (see pictures below and on the next page).

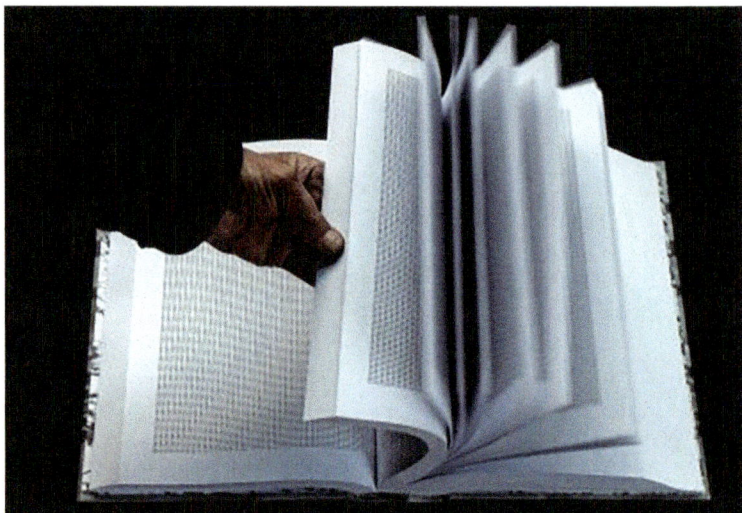

Images credit: Rina Castelnuova

And it takes just a few seconds to read the whole book. More art than literature, the book consists of a single word "JEW" in tiny type, printed six million times to signify the number of Jews killed during the Holocaust.

"When you look at this at a distance, you don't tell whether it is upside down or right side up, you can't tell what is here; it looks like a pattern," says Phil Chernofsky, the author. "That's how the Nazis viewed their victims. These are not individuals, these are not people, they are just a mass that we have to exterminate."

Chernofsky is the educational director of the Orthodox Union's Israel Centre in Jerusalem. The idea for the book came to him in the late 1970's at the Yeshiva of Central Queens in Kew Gardens Hills in Queens. He was teaching math, science and Jewish studies and one year he was asked to do something interesting for Holocaust Remembrance Day.

"I gave the students blank paper, and I said, *'No talking for the next 30 minutes',*" recalls Mr. Chernofsky, 65, who grew up in Crown Heights, Brooklyn, and moved to Israel 32 years ago. "I said, *'I want you to write the word Jew as many times as you can, no margins, just pack them in, just take another paper and another paper until I say stop'.* We added up the whole class. It was 40,000."

The concept is not entirely original. Many decades ago eighth graders in a small town in Tennessee decided to collect 6 million paper clips! However, many Jewish leaders have embraced the book.

But this blog is not about the Holocaust or Chernofsky's effort. The book, though published in August 2013, had been drawn into focus by historians and the Jewish community because 20th January 2017 was the 75th anniversary of the **Wannsee Conference.**

This conference was a meeting of 15 high-ranking Nazi party and German government officials to discuss and coordinate the function of all involved government organizations, to implement what they called **Final Solution of the Jewish Question. Final Solution** was the code name for the systematic, deliberate, physical annihilation of the European Jews. SS General Reinhardt Heydrich was in charge. He indicated that approximately 11,000,000 Jews in Europe would fall under the provisions of the **Final Solution.**

What is fascinating is the clinical, and yet brutal manner in which the implementation of the program was discussed by the group. At one point the group spent a lot of time defining who a Jew is!

The 20th century has gone down in history as the most brutal as far as genocide is concerned. The pogroms conducted in various parts of the world –by heavy weights like Hitler, Mao Ze-Dong and Stalin to relatively minor thugs like Augusto Pinochet - have exterminated millions of innocent people. According to Piero Scaruffi, Italian scientist and lecturer, the casualty of war from 1860 to date, including the Syrian conflict (so far) has exceeded 175 million.

The world is a tapestry torn and the rend will echo through centuries to come and shame civilized people everywhere.

ABOUT THE ILLUSTRATOR

The cover, the section dividers and most of the cartoons were designed by Avijit Sarkar.

Avijit is an extraordinary individual who combines in him talents wide and varied.

He was the professor of Mathematics and software at a University in India. He spent over two decades in the software industry.

He is a concert musician and has given thousands of performances in a career spanning four decades.

He is a writer, actor, artist, and puppeteer. He raises funds for charities through his concerts and devotes a lot of time on his new brainchild—a digital magazine called "The Mind Creative", which is published every month.

He lives in Sydney, Australia.

CPSIA information can be obtained
at www.ICGtesting.com
Printed in the USA
LVOW06s2341201117
557112LV00030B/772/P